A Spirituality of the Road

A Spirituality of the Road

David J. Bosch

Introduction by Cornelius J. Dyck

Institute of Mennonite Studies
Missionary Studies No. 6

Wipf & Stock
PUBLISHERS
Eugene, Oregon

Wipf and Stock Publishers
199 W 8th Ave, Suite 3
Eugene, OR 97401

A Spirituality of the Road
By Bosch, David J.
Copyright©1979 by Bosch, David J.
ISBN: 1-57910-795-8
Publication date 10/26/2001
Previously published by Herald Press, 1979

Contents

Introduction

Many Christians in North America are showing a new concern for spirituality in recent years. The social concerns of the late sixties and early seventies have, it seems, given way to a more inner-directed search for meaning and faith. For some this may be no more than the swing of a pendulum phenomenon from activism to passivism in the aftermath of the Vietnam War, but for many it seems to reflect the longing for deeper biblical and moral roots in the face of the baffling social and political problems.

The decision to focus the spring 1978 sessions of the Mennonite Missionary Study Fellowship (MMSF) on the theme "A Spirituality of the Road" grew from a concern to help those engaged in this search, hoping to lead away from a false kind of spirituality which is content with inwardness alone at the expense of active discipleship lived in the here and now.

The planners of the sessions were not disappointed in their expectations. Based on a study of the Apostle Paul's life and work as reflected in his second letter to the

Corinthians, David J. Bosch brought to these presentations his broad experience as a missionary and churchman, together with profound theological insight and a modest, unassuming spirit that went right to the heart of issues of spirituality with words of both indictment and comfort. While the focus of 2 Corinthians and these lectures is on the missionary situation, the insights shared speak to every Christian concerned for faithfulness. The author rejects a self-seeking, personally selfish spirituality, and in place of the Pilgrim's Progress model on the one hand, or the Jonah model on the other, unequivocally advocates as a third model that of the cross, which is sensitive to both the misery of man and the glory of God.

Dr. David J. Bosch is well known in church circles for his missionary and ecumenical contributions, for his courageous and gentle spirit. He is the editor of *Missionalia*, and Professor of Theology at the University of South Africa in Pretoria. His five presentations at the MMSF sessions were most warmly received, and are commended to all who would grow in the life of the Spirit.

The MMSF is an informally organized group of people meeting annually under the sponsorship of the Institute of Mennonite Studies to reflect on issues relating to Christian mission. In addition to manifest gratitude to Dr. Bosch, appreciation is expressed here to Wilbert R. Shenk and Robert L. Ramseyer for help in planning the sessions and to Suzanne Keeney Lind for her skill in helping to bring the manuscript to press.

Cornelius J. Dyck, Director
Institute of Mennonite Studies
Elkhart, Indiana

1

A Spirituality of the Road

(2 Corinthians 1:1-4; 11:16-31)

I confess that the word "spirituality" has always caused me a degree of uneasiness. Perhaps this has to do with the idea I, and apparently many others as well, have always had about what spirituality seems to mean. By and large, I would guess, most people identify it almost exclusively with what is also known as our "devotional life." And this is always a sensitive area.

Some fourteen years ago the United Presbyterian Church sent its missionaries who were on furlough a questionnaire about the problems they experienced in their overseas work. In one category in the questionnaire the missionaries were asked to indicate in which of the following nine areas they were experiencing difficulties: (1) pursuing devotional life, (2) having friends with whom hair can be let down, (3) doubts over their call, (4) severe anxiety, (5) periods of depression, (6) alcohol, (7) sexual temptations, (8) theological doubts or ambiguities,

(9) fear least they lose their Christian principles.

I think you can guess which one of the nine came out top: almost every missionary admitted having problems in pursuing a satisfactory devotional life! Let us be careful, however, and not deduce too much from this confession. After all, to admit that your devotional life is not quite what it should be counts in your favor. It is a sign of spirituality to admit that you are not as spiritual as you would like to be, and, of course, it is a sign of lack of spirituality, or hypocrisy, to suggest that you do not have any difficulties in this area.

The same does not apply to the other areas in that questionnaire. We are expected to admit problems in the area of devotional life. We are not expected, as missionaries at least, to admit that we sometimes have to fight sexual temptations. Neither, apparently, are presidential candidates expected to make such admissions! You will remember that Jimmy Carter discovered this following a *Playboy* interview several years ago.

The same applies to other areas in the questionnaire. Missionaries are *not* supposed to have doubts over their call, nor to suffer from severe anxiety or periods of depression, nor to have problems with alcohol. Neither should they need somebody with whom hair could be let down; after all, they ought to take their troubles to the Lord! And if they are really spiritual people, so the belief goes, they will not have these problems anyhow.

I have to admit, though, that I experience some difficulties with the U.P.C. questionnaire. The nine items listed are not all necessarily comparable on the same level. Thus, when I, in preparing for this conference, compiled a questionnaire for Mennonite missionaries, I left out items 4, 5, 6, and 9 from the Presbyterian list and substituted several others for them, namely (1) fatigue, possibly due to too heavy a load or being overwhelmed by responsibilities; (2) a feeling of being useless and/or not properly appreciated; (3) relationships with fellow missionaries; (4) relationships with national Christians; (5) homesickness; and (6) family problems.

Even with this wider mix of possibilities, the replies I received were very similar to those to the Presbyterian questionnaire. Of the twenty-three Mennonites who re-plied to this specific question, twelve listed pursuing de-votional life as their major difficulty, whereas six others gave it a second place. Only one other item got more than two first places: fatigue, which five missionaries thought was their major problem. Apparently, then, Mennonites, like Presbyterians, admit that they are not as spiritual as they would like to be.

All this seems to support the view that the missionary is supposed to become less and less worldly. The only worldliness he is allowed to have is to experience some difficulty in becoming more and more otherworldly.

I am increasingly experiencing difficulties with this view of spirituality. Spirituality or devotional life seems to mean withdrawal from the world, charging my bat-tery, and then going out into the world. The image is of an automobile which runs on batteries only. The bat-teries are charged for so many hours during the night and then the automobile runs so many miles during the day until the batteries become too weak to pull the car. For more mileage one would have to charge the batteries for a longer period of time. Transferred to the spiritual sphere, this means: so many minutes of spiritual exercise will give me so much mileage for the day that follows.

And if I find that I am run down before evening, this simply means that I have to spend more time in the morning charging my spiritual battery.

In this view, then, my "true" Christian life consists of those so-called spiritual moments, away from the hustle and bustle of ordinary life. To be sure, all that hubbub is actually anti-spiritual, because it taps my stored-up spiritual resources, it drains my spiritual power away, it is a threat to my spirituality. I would, therefore, much rather live on angels' food only and have as little as possible to do with the things of this world.

Lesslie Newbigin has called this view the "Pilgrim's Progress Model."[1]: the emphasis is on a decisive break with the world and a flight from the "wicked city." In this model the world is primarily seen as a threat, as a source of contagion from which the Christian must keep himself free. To be saved means, in essence, to be saved *from* this world; spirituality means otherworldliness.

The basic problem with this view of spirituality is that it is docetic. It is based on the idea that matter is essentially evil. We could also call it Monophysite because the Christ of this spirituality has only one nature, the divine.

I believe, however, that spirituality has to be redefined along different lines. And we need this redefinition before we can proceed any further; otherwise, we would not know what we are talking about.

It will, naturally, not be possible to give a comprehensive definition of true spirituality at this stage. The parameters of our definition will only gradually take shape as we proceed. I suggest that we do this by looking closely at Paul's second letter to the Corinthians which, I believe, is, by any standards, the best case study in missionary spirituality that has ever been published.

Yet, even before looking more closely at a number of key passages from 2 Corinthians, we ought to attempt to give a very general and preliminary outline of what we understand by spirituality.

Fundamental to any definition of spirituality is that it can never be something that can be isolated from the rest of our existence, as the battery-operated car metaphor suggests. "Flesh" and "spirit" in the Bible do not refer to two segments of our lives, the one outward and worldly, the other inward and otherworldly, as though we are spiritual when we pray and worldly when we work. No, flesh and spirit refer to two modes of existence, two life orientations. Being spiritual means being in Christ, whether we pray or walk or work. Spirituality is not contemplation over against action. It is not a flight from the world over against involvement in the world.

The "Pilgrim's Progress Model" therefore does not adequately describe what spirituality means because its point of departure is noninvolvement, escape from the world. It has to be supplemented by what Newbigin has called the "Jonah Model": not fleeing from the city but being sent by God into the heart of the city and its turmoil.

More precisely, it is not a case of one model supplementing the other, for the two are absolutely indivisible. The involvement in this world should lead to a deepening of our relationship with and dependence on God, and the deepening of this relationship should lead to increasing involvement in the world. Mother Teresa and her Missionaries of Charity in Calcutta are a shining example of this. Touching the poorest of the poor, she says, means touching the body of Christ. Pouring out our love on

people in selfless dedication is a form of prayer. We do
not stop doing the one thing before we begin with the
other. Spirituality is all-pervading.

But to maintain this view of spirituality is one of the
most difficult things to do. And if I am not mistaken, it is
more difficult for Protestants than Catholics. As children
of the Reformation, we have grown up in a tradition
which has tended to view God and man as competitors
for our love and devotion. We have sometimes emphasized the glory of God so much that one came to
think that God can only be glorified at the expense of
man. I know that this distortion was never the intention,
but this is the way it has often worked in practice, in spite
of the clear teaching of Scripture to the contrary (cf. Matthew 22:37-40; 1 John 4:20). This distortion has allowed
a certain blend of Pietism to develop and flourish in
Protestantism, a Pietism which could close its eyes to the
misery of people as long as God would be glorified—as
though it were possible to glorify God without having
compassion on people!

Of late, of course, the situation has changed dra-
matically. Many denominations have discovered their
tragic failure in love. They have come to the realization
that countless church councils down through the
centuries had met to discuss the correct formulations of
the orthodox faith; yet never has a council been con-
vened to discuss the implications of the orthodox love
(Matthew 22:37-40). Now their eyes have been opened
to this missing dimension in their ministry and they are
trying to make up for this neglect. In doing so, the pendulum has, however, often swung completely in the opposite direction. We seem to remain Monophysites, of
one type or the other; previously, we recognized only the

divine in Christ, now we see only the human. Where spirituality used to be defined exclusively as a flight from the world, it is now being defined exclusively as involvement in the world. Where church and world used to be neatly distinguished one from the other, there is now a complete absence of any tension between church and world. The gospel has a complete absence of any tension between church and world. The gospel has become a completely secular message, whereas it used to be entirely religious. The idea of spirituality has either been dropped completely or it has come to be synonymous with secular humanism.

How do we get out of this difficulty? Are we obliged to make a choice here? Often our remedy is to suggest a nice balance between the two: not too much nor too little of either. So much flight from the world coupled with so much involvement in the world will make everything run smoothly. This balance may be just a new form of self-deception. The Lund meeting of "Faith and Order" (1952) recognized this and therefore quite correctly said that the church was always and at the same time "called out of the world and sent into the world." These are not two separate movements but one. The idea is therefore not one of balance but rather of tension. It is not a case of the establishment of an equilibrium. Rather, the church's being called out of the world sends her into the world; her being sent into the world calls her out of the world.

We therefore have to repeat that it is not enough to supplement the Pilgrim's Progress Model with the Jonah Model. Both have to be superseded by a third model, that of the cross. The cross is, in one sense, a sign of total identification with the world: Jesus was never more worldly than on the cross. In another sense it is a sign of radical separation from the world: Jesus never stood over against the world more clearly than here. And spirituality is both of these at the same time.[2]

It seems to me that especially Western peoples experience difficulties here. During my previous visit to the United States, in 1965, I often saw glimpses of Martin Luther King's protest marches on television. One night, as I was watching television with a white American couple, we saw the whole group of marchers all of a sudden kneel down in the street and pray. I remember the white Americans saying to me that they thought that was artificial, something calculated to create effect. It was clear, though, that for King this was genuine and natural. The trouble with us Westerners is that usually the pious are not politically inclined and the politically inclined are not pious. Politics and prayer do not mix! So, deep down we remain dualists, true to our Greek spiritual ancestors. It took us many, many centuries to come to the realization that man could not be subdivided into a *psyche* and a *soma*, that many illnesses involved both the one and the other. Although we thought we had really made tremendous progress in describing certain sicknesses as "psychosomatic," this double word revealed that we have not really succeeded in overcoming our dichotomic thinking. Neither have we succeeded in overcoming this dichotomy in our theology. That is why we so easily make caricatures of one another. Members of one group are told that they are selling out the gospel because of their world-affirming attitude; the second group is accused of being obscurantist and irrelevant because of fleeing from the hard realities of life, while a third group tries to concoct a well-balanced cocktail Christianity in which so many spoonsful of Bible study and so many ounces of prayer are kneaded into the dough of their natural existence. In reality, however, our most menial activities may be permeated with the truest piety and our most devout prayers may be utterly worldly.

Too often missionaries use prayer as an escape from our responsibilities. We say so easily, when we have had a serious problem, "I have prayed about it, and now I leave it in God's hands." This appears to be very pious and submissive, but it may, in fact, be just a cover-up for our unwillingness to face realities. Or it may happen, at other times, that two colleagues, after some misunderstanding, decide to pray about it. Praying is, of course, commendable and even necessary. But when praying about it becomes a kind of magic formula, a panacea, according to the slogan "prayer changes things," then true spirituality has been exchanged for superstition. And too often such colleagues part company without anything really changed. Even in our most pious moments we remain sinners, prone to egoism. We then use our prayers merely as gimmicks to obtain divine sanction for our own blueprints. It is said that most auto accidents are due to egoism. The same is true of most prayer accidents.

We are, then, in need of a new understanding of spirituality—an understanding that is both deeper and broader than most of what we have had so far. This is especially true of the missionary and more specifically of the missionary today. The time has passed when missionaries were regarded by others (and possibly even by themselves!) as spiritual giants. Too often, in the past, they have tried to hide their shortcomings, perhaps totally unconsciously, under all kinds of impressive external trappings. This image does not work anymore. The missionary of today is perhaps the most exposed person in the world. It is not our intention to enter into a discussion of the moratorium issue, but we will not be able to reflect on missionary spirituality unless we keep that issue constantly in our minds.

Indeed, the validity of what the missionary is and stands for is doubted, not only in the countries of the Third World, but also in his home country, if he comes from the West. Some years ago an American missionary in Korea complained as follows: "In my father's day coming home was a kind of triumph. The missionary was a hero. Today he is an anti-hero. Even in Christian churches I am eyed askance as a throwback to a more primitive era . . ."[3]

Now, if the validity of the missionary enterprise is under suspicion both at home and abroad, it seems almost inevitable that the missionary himself will soon be tormented by doubts and ask himself whether there is any point in going on. Two weeks before his recent death, Max Warren, for many years secretary of the Church Missionary Society in Britain, wrote the following words to the General Secretary of the International Association for Mission Studies: "There is a terrible failure of nerve about the missionary enterprise. There is doubt as to its authenticity today, and a widespread misunderstanding of history."[4]

This is just one voice in many reflecting the general malaise about the missionary mandate today. One reaction has been the decision of the Executive Committee of the International Association for Mission Studies to devote its fourth conference to the theme "Credibility and Spirituality in Mission."

It may be of interest that Max Warren, in the letter I have just quoted from, added that the only Christian who had not lost their nerve were to be found among the most conservative groups, especially in North America. I have a slight problem with Warren here, for he appears to suggest that the only alternative to loss of nerve is no loss of nerve. I do not think this distinction is subtle enough. We cannot counteract the widespread loss of nerve with some tough affirmations as though that would settle the issue once for all. No, the missionary enterprise is, by virtue of its very nature, always in dispute. In those periods of history in which it was hardly ever challenged at all, it was, in effect, permanently exposed to the mortal danger of ceasing to transmit the Christian faith and of transmitting a religion, or a culture, or an ideology instead.

What I am rather haltingly trying to say here will, I hope, become clearer from a study of Paul's second letter to the Corinthians. If ever a missionary enterprise were in dispute and a missionary challenged, it was in Corinth. Here I see one of the most remarkable similarities between Paul's situation and ours, for in saying that we are ἀγνοούμενοι, "unknown men" (2 Corinthians 6:9), he is, in fact, saying that he and his fellow missionaries are being rejected and discredited. He is not saying that they are unknown in the literal sense of the word. After all, he adds, "whom all men know"! The point is that those others prefer not to take notice of Paul and his associates. They are, instead, being studiously ignored and denigrated. That all this did not, in Paul's case, lead to despondency and self-pity is one of the central messages of 2 Corinthians. That Paul could, in fact, triumph in those very circumstances is a sign of the authenticity of his spirituality and a challenge to ours.

Paul's spirituality was, however, never a kind of permanent attribute, a possession or achievement; it was renewed again and again from within. As he writes to the Corinthians, chapter after chapter, it develops, unfolds, deepens, and matures. Never fixed and finished, it is a spirituality that journeys from stage to stage. Paul never "arrives," at least not before he reaches his true and final destination. His is not a spirituality of the monastery but of the road.[5]

Still, there are no trace of feverishness and agitation in Paul's spirituality. He isn't driving himself relentlessly, in spite of all the many external pressures on him, in spite of what he himself refers to as the responsibility that weighs on him every day, namely his concern for all the congregations (2 Corinthians 11:28). I have said that my questionnaire to Mennonite missionaries has revealed that, apart from difficulty in "pursuing [their] devotional life," there is especially one other area which is causing them problems: "fatigue, possibly due to too heavy a load or being overwhelmed by responsibilities." If I had to fill in this questionnaire myself, I would also have wavered between these two items, not being quite sure which one of them constitutes the major problem for me. Unless I am mistaken, however, Paul experienced things differently, for we hear him saying: "Hard-pressed on every side, we are never hemmed in; bewildered, we are never at our wits' end; hunted, we are never abandoned to our fate; struck down, we are not left to die" (4:8, 9). And again: "Dying, we still live on; disciplined by suffering, we are not done to death; in our sorrows we have always cause for joy" (6:9, 10). So there remains an atmosphere of all-pervading calmness in Paul's ministry.

We desperately need this message, for missionaries face danger on two levels: overactivity and loss of discipline. I will address the latter first. There is the terrible temptation to relax far too much, to take it easy. Because of our natural inclinations, it does not take much to cause our energy to flag and our enthusiasm to dwindle. Often the societies in which we as missionaries live tend to strengthen this inclination. It is undeniable that for many missionaries it is far easier to remain on the mission field than to return to their home countries where competition is much stiffer. For many it would be a sacrifice to return home. So often we follow the way of least resistance and stay on the field. For example, the sermons we ordained missionaries preach too often reflect shabby preparation that would never be tolerated at home. I fear the same applies to other areas of missionary activity as well.

Some years ago a study was made of 118 case histories of first-term missionary failures. The study included reports from eleven mission boards, large and small, and represented all major fields. Gordon Frazer, who undertook the study, discovered that there were some twelve main categories of reasons for these missionary casualities. "Incapacity or unwillingness to formulate and carry out a satisfactory daily detail of operation" was responsible for 10 percent of the first-term failures. Other related categories included "carelessness or evasiveness in the preparation of . . . reports" and "inability to maintain a satisfactory standard of . . . tidiness to the extent that there was a reflection on the work of the mission." Together these three categories were responsible for 22 percent, or almost one quarter, of the failures. I suppose these three categories could be subsumed under one: only, lack of self-discipline.

The study I have just referred to dealt only with first-term failures, but I suspect that the problem might prove to be even more serious if we made an in-depth study of those missionaries who remained on the field. Many are in severe ruts, seemingly finding it impossible to get out. Someone has said: "Beware of ruts. They are, in fact, shallow graves!" Many years ago an elderly Chinese gentleman said to a young American missionary on board ship, en route for the first time to the mission field: "Your first term out there you will be a Christian missionary. Your second term you will be a Christian. Your third term you will be just another American enjoying life abroad!" Of how many of us is this true? Don't we also just coast along comfortably, having long ago lost our enthusiasm and idealism, the sparkle in the eye which we had when we first went out?

The first danger we face, then, is the loss of self-discipline and slipping into a comfortable and well-oiled rut.

The second danger is equally serious. It is the danger of overactivity and overinvolvement. We may be so caught up in the hectic activities of development work, social work, teaching, preaching, health care, or administration, that we not only lose our perspective, but sometimes even our sanity. We may be so conscious of everything that is still undone, so conscious of our own responsibilities, that we drive ourselves on and on relentlessly and in this process lose the joy of the Christian life. So often life is, for us, such a desperate struggle against evil, injustice, darkness, squalor, that we allow ourselves to be robbed of the peace of mind which is a precondition for all our involvement. Our activities then easily become divorced from the tender intimate love which gave them birth and which ought to remain their mainspring. We feel that we are being pushed to do, to achieve, to give, in order to earn some degree of credibility and justification for our presence, but in this process we ourselves get so buried under many deeds that people find it extremely difficult to see who we are. We seem to find it impossible to say no to people, for this might be misinterpreted. So we desperately keep on working for acceptance by others, assuming that this is the only way in which we can justify our presence. In this process, however, we run the risk of neglecting the central doctrine that our justification is by faith, not works, and that we do not need to earn our acceptance by others.

Those, then, are the two dangers facing us. We can either content ourselves with the rut we're in and have complete peace of mind about it or we can urge ourselves on madly and relentlessly. There is a third way, however: that of living in a gentle tension between giving ourselves in full surrender to our fellowman, yet at the same time enjoying the peace of the Lord. The Jesus who said, "If anyone wishes to be a follower of mine, he must leave self behind; he must take up his cross and come with me" (Matthew 16:24) was the same One who said: "Come to me, all whose work is hard, whose load is heavy; and I will give you relief" (Matthew 11:28). It is that simultaneous "double movement" again: going into the world and coming out of the world.

The Apostle Paul knew this secret, for he could genuinely take pride in his weakness. This weakness is no euphemism for sheer laziness or fear of involvement, as it sometimes is with us, but the positive acceptance of our own limits and incapacities and our trust that the Lord does not mind us being what we are. One person prayed at night: "For what I have today left undone that I could have done, may the Lord make me truly thankful!" Of course, you cannot pray this when you have not given yourself as you should have. But you *can* pray it if you know deep down in your heart that you could only have tackled those still undone things at a price which would have been too high.

Indeed, the costs involved in being a missionary today are so high that it is inevitable that many vitally important things will be left undone. To be a stranger and at the same time at home in another society, to become part of another country and people, to surrender the ties with home and family, to learn another language until it becomes your own, to identify with the struggles and needs of another people—all this and much more is no easy matter and not something anybody should lightly take. Nevertheless, in taking on these responsibilities, one can only do it in the way Paul did it, or risk being plowed under in one way or the other.

Naturally, if we study Paul's second letter to the Corinthians, we should guard against using this facilely as a kind of blueprint for present-day missionary spirituality. The experiences of Paul and his fellow laborers were conditioned by time and circumstances very different from those we may be facing. We cannot apply them to our situation on a one-to-one basis. Yet we may recognize enough of ourselves and our own problems in them to help us on our way today. Like Paul and his co-workers, we are not better than poets of earthenware containing an invaluable treasure; like him, we know that the transcendent power which does indeed manifest itself in what we do as missionaries does not come from us, but from God alone (4:7).

Hawkers or Rejoicing Captives?

(2 Corinthians 1:15—2:17; 11:1-6, 12-15)

The central theme of Paul's second letter to the Corinthians is the legitimacy of his apostolic ministry, which he defends against the accusations of certain sham "apostles" who have infiltrated the church of Corinth. Or, stated differently, one finds the dominant theme as the search for true Christian missionary spirituality. This focus explains the intensely personal character of this letter. It is striking that discussions about doctrinal matters are almost totally absent here, which explains why 2 Corinthians, in the development of Christian theology, never played a role comparable to that of Romans, Galatians, or 1 Corinthians.

Somehow, though, today's missionary may in many ways feel closer to 2 Corinthians than to some of the other Pauline letters. Here is a man very much like us, no giant, in fact, in the eyes of his opponents, the very opposite of a giant—a very vulnerable man, misunderstood on all sides, even by the very people he has led to Christ.

We do not with any certainty know who Paul's opponents were. From his first letter we know that there were several mutually opposing parties in Corinth, the Pauline party, the Apollos party, the Cephas party, and the Christ party (1 Corinthians 1:12). Possibly his opponents in 2 Corinthians were related to one of these groups and possibly they had only arrived in Corinth since the first letter had been written. From the unexplained references and allusions in 2 Corinthians it sometimes appears that they must have been Gnostics, or, perhaps, a group of Hellenistic Jewish itinerant preachers. For our purposes, however, their identity is not so terribly important. What *is* important, though, is their understanding of the Christian gospel and, more specifically, of Paul's ministry. Paul had no doubt that they were proclaiming "another Jesus," and "a gospel different from the gospel . . . [the Corinthians had] already accepted" (11:4). He referred to them as "sham-apostles, crooked in all their practices, masquerading as apostles of Christ" (11:13), the agents of Satan who himself "masquerades as an angel of light" (11:14, 15).

One is tempted to say that Paul's attitude here is typical of many modern intolerant evangelists who identify their cause and approach with Christ's and condemn everybody whose emphasis differs from their own. Yet clearly this case is different, as we may discover when we compare this letter with the one to the Philippians, where Paul writes: "Some, indeed, proclaim Christ in a jealous and quarrelsome spirit; others proclaim him in true goodwill, and these are moved by love for me; they know that it is to defend the Gospel that I am where I am. But the others, moved by personal rivalry, present Christ from mixed motives, meaning to stir up fresh trouble for me as I lie in prison. What does it matter? One way or another, in pretence or sincerity, Christ is set forth, and for that I rejoice" (Philippians 1:15-18).

I have heard missionaries say, when they feel rejected and opposed by others: "Well, I just have to accept this as part of my cross. We know, after all, that Christ's messengers will suffer for the stand they take." This sounds terribly pious but need not be so. Too often the opposition we experience is in no way related to the gospel we purport to proclaim but simply to our own human selves. Paul, however, could distinguish between suffering caused by one's own stubbornness and sinfulness on the one hand, and suffering which flowed from one's loyalty to Jesus Christ on the other. The total thrust of the second letter to the Corinthians is that much more is at stake here than the idiosyncrasies of the apostle himself.

We will come back, again and again, to the controversy between Paul and the false apostles. At this stage I intend just to highlight some of the accusations they voiced against Paul. Apparently these people arrived in Corinth equipped with letters of recommendation and were soon able to impress the believers there with their superior religion. They claimed to be Jews and "servants of Christ" (11:22); they were excellent orators and boasted about having received special visions and revelations as proof of the fact that they were superspiritual men. They accused Paul of fickleness because he had changed his plans about a visit to Corinth (1:17); they accused him of cunning and distortion (4:2), of preaching a veiled or muddled gospel (4:3), of being

brave at a distance but feeble when face to face with the
Corinthians and a poor speaker (10:1, 10), of being
morally weak (10:2), without the marks of an apostle
(12:12) and without any evidence that Christ was speak-
ing through him (13:3). Above all else, they judged him
to be a weakling, of which his poor health gives ample
proof. And the Christ he proclaimed was a crucified,
feeble, dull creature without any heavenly glory.

The comparisons between Paul and these "superlative
apostles" (as he mockingly refers to them in 11:5 and
12:11) found willing ears among the Christians in
Corinth. A wedge was being driven between them and
Paul and also between them and Christ.

At an early stage in his defense Paul takes up the matter of the change in his itinerary which caused him not to
visit Corinth as originally planned (1:15—2:14). In a
beautiful passage he explains that this change was in no
way due to fickleness, as the Corinthians were led to
believe, but out of consideration for them (1:23). Not
wanting to impose upon them, he had sent Titus as his
representative. We could say that he adopted a low
profile in the matter, allowing the Corinthians to come to
terms with the issues without dictating to them (1:23).

All these changes in his plans, far from being due to in-
decision and arbitrariness, are due, he says, to Christ's
guidance. He himself is no more than a captive who is
continually being led about in Christ's triumphal
procession (2:14). The metaphor is not absolutely clear
but seems to refer to the march of triumph of a victorious
Roman general who parades his captives and booty
through the packed streets of Rome (cf. also Colossians
2:15). Usually, of course, such captives are a sorry sight
and form a wretched procession of despondent and spirit-

less people. But here Paul presents the picture of a paradox—one of the many in this letter—for this captive is rejoicing! He gives the glory to God for the hardships of his captivity! Not that he is unaware of the seriousness of the situation. In fact, he has taken up the same theme in his first letter to the Corinthians and has even pursued it a bit further there: the captives are not only parading through the streets of Rome but are actually on their way to the Colosseum. So he says: "It seems to me God has made us apostles the most abject of mankind. We are like men condemned to death in the arena, a spectacle to the whole universe—angels as well as men" (1 Corinthians 4:9, 10).

The decisive point is, however, that Paul does not simply accept all this condition as an inescapable fate; he joyfully endorses it. We should be careful, however, not to interpret this as triumphalism or cheap euphoria. One of the crucial differences between him and the sham-apostles is precisely that they interpret the Christian faith in triumphalistic categories, whereas, for Paul, it means exactly the opposite.

All of a sudden, then, Paul changes the metaphor, typical of the lively style of his letters. He and his fellow laborers are not only the captives in the procession, but also an aroma scattered by the incense-bearers who used to accompany such triumphal processions (2:14, 15). This fragrance of "the knowledge of God" is in this way "revealed and spread about everywhere." It is, on the one hand, a fragrance that rises up to God for His glory ("incense offered by Christ to God," v. 15), but, on the other hand, it also has a decisive impact on all those who come in touch with it (vv. 15, 16). We will return to this latter effect of the fragrance. At this stage we merely

want to point out that Paul frequently links the idea of
the fragrance of incense with that of sacrifice (cf.
Ephesians 5:2; Philippians 4:18). So the two metaphors
that are intertwined here are actually saying one and the
same thing: a rejoicing captive *is* a fragrant sacrifice.

Not that the apostle regards himself as *capable* of, or
qualified for, being this *quality*! On the contrary, when
he considers the momentous challenge before him, he
becomes aware of his own inadequacy. Who, he says, is
equal to such a calling? (v. 16). This is a rhetorical question to which the answer can only be: "Nobody."
Surprisingly, however, there *are* people who believe that
they are worthy and capable of being Christ's servants.
Paul refers to them as "hawkers" (2:17) or people "who
handle God's message as if it were cheap merchandise"
(Good News Bible). They are the sham-apostles who, in
fact, adulterate the gospel in their efforts to make their
message acceptable. Typical of the itinerant hawker or
peddler is the element of bickering in all his business
transactions. The real value of his merchandise is of no
consequence to him; the only thing he is interested in is
what he himself can get out of it. He will undersell a
competitor but often only after having diluted the
product he is offering for sale. In this way his profit
remains guaranteed.

What Paul says here is a challenge to our missionary
methods as well as to our spirituality. It took a long time
for the Christian mission from the West to unlearn the
triumphalism of the hawker. The optimism and the
military terminology that were, for so long, typical of the
missionary enterprise of both Roman Catholics and
Protestants, are indicative of this mentality. At the World
Missionary Conference in Edinburgh (1910), to take but

one example, the terms that were used again and again included the following: soldiers, forces, advance, army, crusade, marching orders, strategy, planning, and many more. To this day we talk about an evangelistic campaign, a crusade, a missionary offensive. And even when we do not use this terminology, our conduct often reveals a comparable mentality. We think in the context of clear-cut answers to every problem. We practice an "answer-theology," says the Japanese theologian Kosuke Koyama.[6] Some time ago a large evangelistic "campaign" was "launched" in a city in India. The posters displayed the message: "Jesus Christ is the answer!" On one of these a student scrawled the words: "Yes, but what was the question?" The typical hawker's mentality is not interested in people's needs and questions but only in his own merchandise—like a typical door-to-door salesman, with his "this-will-solve-all-your-problems" approach.

We, too, have been tempted to present the gospel as a happy-ending religion. A missionary on furlough complains: "Our audiences at home demand Hollywood endings." The problem is that too often we have spoiled them by supplying them with just that. The missionary enterprise has become indissolubly fused with the ethic of capitalism. In everything we undertake we think in the categories of success, of yield and dividends, and we have transposed that to our missionary enterprise as well. So we feel terribly embarrassed when we cannot report tangible results, when miracles do not happen on our mission field the way they do happen on others', when the spectacular appears to be completely absent in our work and only the dreariness seems to be in evidence. A Dutch missionary to Pakistan tells of his frustration when he is time and time again confronted at home with the question: "How many Muslims have you already converted to Christianity?"

The theologian Koyama, to whom I referred earlier, says it is natural for us to want to have efficient control of a situation. We do not like to be baffled by circumstances. We want our religion to be an integral part of a given society; it should be an institution of society alongside the school system, the civil service, and the army. We want, Koyama says, to domesticate the cross by providing it with a handle which will make it manageable, so we can carry it about like a lunchbox. "With a nourishing and well-filled lunchbox in our hands we can whistle and light-footedly follow Jesus, 'from victory unto victory!' ... We can be and will remain resourceful. If necessary, we can even walk ahead of Jesus instead of 'follow him.' "[7] Resourceful people always know exactly what to do; they do not seek help from others. They are not, like Paul, captives in the triumphal procession, but are themselves the victorious, having placed themselves at the head of the procession. They see Christ at work only where outward glory, heavenly power, and imposing signs are clearly manifested. An unmistakable euphoria emanates from their activities.

All this impressive spirituality is, however, according to Paul, utterly futile. Over against this he develops a missionary theology and practice in which ecstatic phenomena and spectacular achievements may never become the proof of being truly sent by Christ.[8] The temptation the missionary faces is the same as the one faced by Jesus: to be a popular Messiah, fitting the expectations of this world. In 2 Corinthians, however, Paul argues that true Christian spirituality is not to be found in the superhuman and the miraculous, but in the commonplace. Our problem is that we have even turned the commonplaces of the gospel into something romantic and folksy. We have provided the cross with a halo and changed the stable of Bethlehem into something idyllic and sentimental. This view misses the terribly mundane and ordinary nature of these images. Likewise, the criteria for missionary service and spirituality are not in magnificent and romantic accomplishments, but in ordinary daily existence. So Paul opposes the impressive arsenal of his opponents with down-to-earth weapons: patience, truth, love, weakness, service, modesty, and respect.[9] Under no circumstances should people be bulldozed with the gospel, for it ceases to be the gospel when foisted upon people. It is possible to be unaggressive and missionary at the same time. It is, indeed, the only way of being truly missionary.

A god who provides all the answers becomes an explicable and comprehensible god, but also ceases to be God. Albert Schweitzer, in recollecting the ten years he taught catechism classes to boys in Strassbourg before the First World War, noted that after the war some of those young men thanked him that he had shown them so clearly that the Christian faith does not explain everything. This awareness enabled them to survive spiritually in the trenches, whereas many others, who were told that Christianity provided all the answers, lost their faith when faced with that which was inexplicable.

After the Second World War a piece of paper was found among the ruins of the Jewish ghetto in Warsaw. It contained the last words of a Jew, Jessel Rakover, as he was preparing himself for the pogrom. Part of it reads as follows:

I believe in you, God of Israel, even if you have tried your
best to dissuade me to believe in you. I believe in your laws,
even if I cannot approve of the way you manage things. . . .
I bow my head before your majesty, but I will not kiss the
rod with which you hit me. . . . I would like to say to you
that at this moment, more even than in any previous period
of our eternal struggle for survival, we, the tortured, the
humiliated, buried alive, burnt alive, insulted, mocked, we,
murdered by the million, that we have the right to know:
until when are you going to allow it to continue? . . . I say
this to you because I believe in you, more than ever before,
because I know now, with absolute certainty, that you are
my God, because you cannot be the God of those whose
deeds are the most horrendous expression of godlessness;
. . . I die in peace, but not appeased; persecuted, but not
enslaved; embittered, but not cynical; a believer, but not
pleading; a man who loves God, but does not say amen to
everything. I have followed God even when he had rejected
me. I have obeyed his command even when he punished me
for that. I have loved him, even when he had flung me
down, tortured me, and made me an object of humilitation
and derision. And these are my last words to you, my angry
God: all this will do you no good. You have done everything
possible to destroy my faith, yet I am dying precisely as I
have lived, saying: "Shma Yishrael, hear, O Israel, the Lord
is our God, one Lord." Into your hands, O God, I commit
my spirit.

This moving document reveals the same kind of spirituality one finds in Paul, in contrast to that of the
"hawkers." Augustine said: "For it is better for them to
find you and leave the question unanswered than to find
the answer without finding you."[10]

Psalm 22 proclaims a similar message. It opens with
the cry of distress: "My God, my God, why hast thou
forsaken me . . .? O my God, I cry in the day-time but
thou dost not answer, in the night I cry but get no respite

..." (vv. 1, 2). Throughout Psalm 22 this question is never muffled nor swept under the table, and there is no answer to this accusing "Why?" Still, immediately after this piercing question the poet continues completely illogically: "And yet thou art enthroned in holiness, thou art he whose praises Israel sings" (v. 3). The poet then continues with his prayers and supplications only to change once more abruptly to a doxology: "I will declare thy fame to my brethren; I will praise thee in the midst of the assembly. Praise him, you who fear the Lord; all you sons of Jacob, do him honor; stand in awe of him, all sons of Israel" (vv. 22, 23).

The same happened with Jeremiah (20:7-9, 14, 18) and with Jesus on the cross. Koyama comments:

> Jeremiah and Jesus place their trust in the forsaking God! Theirs is no longer the faith built upon God's obvious answer. They believed in God even though God did not answer! ... Here we do not see an answer-theology. We see instead a relationship-theology.[11]

For the church, for the missionary, this means turning our backs on any form of human-success thinking. I will never forget the remarks of a black South African, when confronted with the question what the church was going to do in view of the unrest in the black townships two years ago. He said: "We are so inveigled with the success ethic that we do not realize that, in some ways, the church was *meant* to be a failing community." Our very success may, in fact, be a sign of our failures, and vice versa. The German missiologist, Walter Freytag, tells of a visit he paid many years ago to a Lutheran mission station in Upper Egypt. At the time of his visit the work had been going on for fifty-two years. The yield of all those years was one convert from Islam who had, however, again disappeared. Yet the missionaries labored on faithfully. And Freytag said that as he stood there, he realized what mission truly was—to praise the Lord Christ among the peoples of the earth, irrespective of the outcome, even in a situation as hopeless as that one.

This understanding is extremely important to the way we modern missionaries go about presenting Christ to the people of other faiths. If we follow the approach of the hawkers in 2 Corinthians we do not communicate the gospel, we transmit a religion, or a culture, or an ideology.[12] The nineteenth-century German theologian Martin Kähler, lifelong friend of the missiologist Gustav Warneck, said that it was of crucial importance to distinguish between "mission" and "propaganda." The latter, he said, meant "making carbon copies of what we are ourselves." I fear that much of our so-called mission work has been just that. It has been a case of justifying one's own religion over against another and the winning of as many new supporters as possible for one's own cause. Our point of departure has been: "We have the truth, we are right, all the rest are wrong." Our global censures of the convictions of others have often been expressed in tones of regrettable shrillness.

Paul so devastatingly criticized in Romans 2:17-21 precisely this attitude of the Jews toward Gentiles. The Jews were confident that they were the ones "to guide the blind, to enlighten the benighted, to train the stupid, and to teach the immature" (vv. 19, 20). Paul's objection was that the Jews, in their arrogance, had blithely annexed and monopolized God's revelation for themselves and had proceeded to take it for granted that, on the basis of this possession, they had arrived in an unassailable position of security in respect to God and man.

In a subsequent chapter, I will come back to this whole issue and attempt to show how, in 2 Corinthians, Paul managed to combine an attitude of modesty and tolerance with a clear conviction about salvation in Christ. At this stage it will have to suffice to point out that such a clear conviction has nothing whatsoever to do with treating the Christian faith as absolute and exclusive on the basis of comparing it with other religions. "We have had enough of this 'divine beauty contest,' " says Koyama.[13] He refers to the imprisoned John the Baptist sending his disciples to Jesus with the question: "Are you the one who is to come, or are we to expect some other?" (Matthew 11:2). It is crucial, Koyama points out, to realize that this very first question on record about the "finality of Christ" was not asked in an air-conditioned university library or the carpeted lounge of a theological seminary, but by a prisoner from within the walls of a prison.

In the same manner the "no other name under heaven granted to men, by which we may receive salvation" (Acts 4:12) was a conviction uttered by two trembling detainees who were not arguing about the absoluteness of the Christian religion, but were gripped by Jesus Christ and *therefore* could not do otherwise. These scriptural testimonies, are in fact, high-voltage passages and we should guard against using them carelessly, lest we electrocute ourselves and others. Is Koyama not right when he says: "It is better to be merciful in the name of the Buddha than to be cruel in the name of Christ. It is better to become a neighbor with a Samaritan theology ... than to desert the beaten victim with Jewish theology ... "?[14]

This testimony suggests that we are ourselves part of the message we proclaim (the subject of the next chapter). In 1 Peter 3:15 we read: "Be always ready with your defence whenever you are called to account for the hope that is in you, but make that defence with modesty and respect." Apparently these Christians are not themselves publicizing their religious commodities as the hawkers are doing. Rather, the pagans are coming to them and asking them to give account—of what?—of the *hope* that is in them! This, then, is what the pagans recognize: these people have a hope we do not have; so let us go to them and find out what it is all about.

Surely this understanding does not suggest that we should never take the initiative in proclaiming Christ. But it does mean that it would be futile to take such an initiative unless people can recognize at least a glimmer of the hope that is in us.

In conclusion and in summary, let us establish the essential difference between Paul and his opponents in Corinth. I believe the opponents were in fact bypassing the cross. This theme will come back to us in many variations as we study this letter. Without the cross the Christian life and faith becomes something obvious and explicable, Jesus becomes an idol whom we can comprehend, predict, and domesticate. But a Jesus who could be mocked, spat on, and stripped is different.

Of course, we have become very good at the game of domesticating even the cross. We may be making all the right noises and saying all the right prayers; we may be solely concerned about "proclaiming Christ crucified" and still remain in the company of the hawkers. We may ostensibly have exchanged the robe of the Pharisee for the tattered garment of the repentant publican and then start thanking God that we are not like the Pharisee. You remember old Screwtape writing to his nephew Wormwood: "You say your patient has become humble ... Well, have you drawn his attention to the fact? Just make him proud of his humility ..."

We know, from the Gospel narratives, that the publican is closer to the kingdom of heaven than the Pharisee. "It is not the healthy that need a doctor, but the sick; I have not come to invite virtuous people, but to call sinners to repentance" (Luke 5:31, 32). But if repentant sinners turn their repentance into a virtue they are back where they were, or rather, they are worse than they were, for now they have developed an immunity against the gospel.

In reading 2 Corinthians, it becomes clear that Paul himself often moved on the very edge of disaster in this respect, for "boasting" or "bragging" is one of the key concepts in this letter. The Greek word for boast occurs more frequently here than in all the other Pauline letters taken together. Paul's opponents boasted about their superiority and compared themselves with him, just like the Pharisee in the parable. Paul's reaction to this was a counterboast. This is a terribly dangerous game and Paul knew it. He nevertheless felt obliged to refute the sham-apostles, not by priding himself, like they did, in his strength, but in his weakness. So he came very near to being a publican in the robes of a Pharisee. The decisive point is, however, that Paul did this with great hesitation and bitter irony. More important, he did this on the basis of the reality of the experience of the grace of Christ in his life and being "enlisted in the service of reconciliation" (5:18).[15]

3

Christ's Ambassadors

(2 Corinthians 3:18; 5:18—6:10)

More than forty years ago the Dutch theologian Hendrik Kraemer wrote a book that was intended as preparatory material for the Tambaram Conference of the International Missionary Council in 1938. In *The Christian Message in a Non-Christian World* Kraemer challenged the relativistic approach to other religions which had become popular at the Jerusalem conference ten years earlier, mainly because of the contribution of the Harvard philosophy professor William Hocking.

In many respects Kraemer followed Emil Brunner in his evaluation of non-Christian religions, as well as displaying some affinity with Karl Barth. For one thing, he was very wary of talking about "similarities" between the Christian faith and other religions. He pointed out that all so-called similarities or points of contact, as they were often called at the time, were at the same time dissimilarities. After a lengthy theological discussion of the whole issue, Kraemer then rather abruptly says:

> One might state this important aspect of the problem of concrete points of contact in this somewhat unusual way: that there is only one point of contact and if that point really exists, then there are many points of contact. This one point of contact is the disposition and the attitude of the missionary. It seems rather upsetting to make the missionary the point of contact. Nevertheless it is true. [16]

I believe that Kraemer stands on firm biblical ground here. In 2 Corinthians 2:15 and 16, as noted earlier, Paul refers to himself and his fellow workers as "the incense offered by Christ to God," as spreading the fragrance of the knowledge of God among all people. And if we really understand the incarnational aspect of the Christian faith, it should only be logical that this be so.

We often call ourselves channels or instruments which God uses to communicate His message to people. Our understanding of such a channel usually is that of a clean water pipe which does nothing but allow an unrestricted flow of water. In order to guarantee this flow, the channel or pipe has to be cleaned regularly. Transposed to the missionary sphere the suggestion seems to be that the message has got to be kept aseptic in the process of communication. It should in no way be contaminated but remain absolutely pure.

In the channel or instrument metaphor, the missionary becomes a mere tool; the idea almost seems to be that it is regrettable that such a tool should be used, but inasmuch as no other means of communication exists, we have to put up with such tools. There is, however, no direct relationship between the instrument and that which it conveys; in fact, the whole idea is for the instrument not to get involved with the contents.

I can appreciate the sentiments behind this kind of thinking, even though the New Testament does not seem to me to understand the missionary as such a disinfected or antiseptic tool who should himself under no circumstances be involved in the communications process. The New Testament metaphor is not the instrument but a branch (John 15). A channel remains unaffected by what flows through it, but a branch has, first of all, to absorb the nutritive power which comes to it from the roots and trunk. It has to make all this a part of itself, and allow itself to be affected and renewed and transformed by that power. Only after having assimilated such energy can the branch impart it to the fruit. The branch is, therefore, itself involved in the process of transmitting nourishment.

This personal involvement comes out especially clearly in 1 Peter (for example, 2:12). The idea behind this verse seems to be that the opponents of the Christians are doing their very best to malign the believers, trying to collect any possible scrap of evidence that might help them prove that the Christians are criminals. Their campaign, however, leads to exactly the opposite. The wind is taken out of their sails, because the behavior of the Christians is such that the opponents cannot find any grounds for censure. On the contrary, they find themselves compelled to give glory to God because of the example of the Christians.

In no New Testament writing, however, is the emphasis on the personal involvement of the Christian as a *part* of the message he proclaims so clearly evident as in 2 Corinthians. Paul's version of the branch metaphor is to call himself and his co-workers "Christ's ambassadors" (5:20). The ambassador is more than just an instrument that carries messages to and from his government. He is not the same as the diplomatic mailbag. He is a personal representative of his government, the very embodiment of the one who sends him.

Because the ambassador's role is so crucial he has to undergo a very careful preparation. The call to be an ambassador is not enough. It therefore always amazes me that many churches and missionary agencies seem to think that the preparation of the missionary is not so terribly important. If he has received a call, that is all that matters. He should go off to the mission field as soon as possible, especially in view of the chronic shortages in personnel and the urgency of the missionary task. Yet, from the New Testament record, one gets a different impression. After Paul's conversion, he disappeared into Arabia, where he spent three years. We know little of that period in his life, but on the basis of the New Testament evidence we may surmise that those years were essentially years of preparation. Paul then spent a short period in Jerusalem and subsequently many more years in his home town of Tarsus. It was only after some fifteen or more years of relative obscurity that he became the missionary we know. In fact, our Lord's own earthly life reveals the same emphasis on preparation. He spent about thirty years in obscurity, while His public ministry lasted three years, at the most.

I often wonder whether our modern mission work would not have proved itself to be vastly different if we had laid a corresponding emphasis on preparation. I am not thinking of a theological preparation only—in Paul's case he had already had that before his conversion!—but also of what we may call a psychological preparation or missionary formation.

It is only in recent decades that the phenomenon of culture shock and its influence on people moving into another culture has been studied in depth. In most cases a Westerner who moves to another culture can, however, protect himself against an excessive exposure to culture shock. He may, for instance, confine his associations to fellow Westerners and also, in a variety of other ways, succeed in creating for himself a little island of home abroad. Not infrequently missionaries try to do exactly that, taking England or America along with them so they only migrate geographically but never psychologically. Whereas the American businessman usually can get away with this, the missionary cannot. For a missionary to isolate himself from his new environment is to destroy whatever he has come to say or to do.

Later we will explore the implications of this exposure for the missionary and his relations to the nationals, but here I am primarily interested in showing how these factors may have a very far-reaching influence on the missionary and his whole psychological and spiritual make-up. His life is one of being constantly exposed. There are the problems of forced togetherness with incompatible personalities, not being able to choose one's own friends—you have just got to accept what you are given—and the lack of privacy.

All this may cause a tremendous strain under which too often we snap. I remember one of the finest and most talented young missionary doctors who came to me because he could not cope with the demands of life in a missionary situation. He said, "You know, in medical school we were only trained to be doctors. There was just no time left for anything but study, study, study. And when we then move into a situation such as this, we discover that we are incomplete and unprepared for life."

It was that young man's salvation that he knew where and how he had failed. Only too often the possible realization of failure is suppressed and then manifests itself in obstinacy and self-righteousness. Small wonder that the same Hendrik Kraemer whom I have quoted earlier once said: "Communities of missionaries are amongst the most difficult ones in the world!" An American missionary in Rhodesia/Zimbabwe wrote home: "The greatest trial so far has come in getting along with our fellow missionaries."

I suppose one of the reasons for this is that, even in our comfortable modern world, it still takes some guts to become a missionary. Not everybody has the courage to go off to another country to do such a difficult job. So missionaries, by and large, tend to be strong personalities, as they themselves would like to put it. The strength of these personalities may reveal itself in the most peculiar ways, though, for missionaries often conjugate the expression "to be firm" as follows: I am firm, you are stubborn, he is pigheaded. The three words have the same factual meaning; they have, however, very different *emotional* meanings.

In 1965 the Missionary Research Library in New York published a report on the reasons why 1409 Protestant missionaries from a large variety of churches and societies had left the field prematurely. One of the questions was, "Did you find living and working with missionary colleagues more or less difficult than with colleagues in the homeland?" Twenty percent of the respondents said that they found cooperation with missionary colleagues easier; 30 percent thought it was much the same; but 45 percent claimed that living and working with fellow missionaries was undoubtedly more difficult. One from this latter group wrote: "It was a terrible shock to see the senior missionaries fighting. My image of a missionary was shattered." These revealing answers remind me of a remark by Mr. Jawaharlal Nehru when he was prime minister of India and he paid his first ever visit to the U.S.A. At a press conference he was asked what he thought about America. He replied, "Well, all I can say is, one should never go to America for the first time!"

One might say the same about a missionary situation: one should never go into it for the first time. Precisely that first encounter with fellow workers may often give us the shock of a cold shower on a winter morning. To make things even worse, the young missionary has often left his or her home church with quite a fanfare. After such an exalted commissioning and good-bye, it is only natural for the young missionary to regard himself as God's special gift to the mission or the young church. He hopes to be received on the field with a comparable flourish of trumpets. Often, however, it seems to the recruit, the missions committee or the young church does not quite appear to know what to do with the new arrival. He begins to feel in the way, to wonder why ever he has come, and to doubt the stories about the chronic shortages of staff. And immediately seeing a thousand things that he could criticize, he can forget that it is he himself who is on trial, not the young church or the mission field.

A. J. Dain says that there are, in fact, three types of missionary recruits. First, there are those whom you could send anywhere at any time, and know that they would make their grade. Second, there are those for whom you must find the right type of work and a congenial atmosphere; you cannot put Miss X with Miss Y, and you cannot put Mr. Z in the situation as it is at that specific station. So you have to do quite a degree of jigsaw puzzling. Third, there are those who cannot safely be used anywhere and who have to return home. Dain continues: "It is the second category that worries me." They usually do not go home but remain as misfits, a liability rather than an asset to the church.[17]

It is difficult for the newcomer to the field to realize that it is not so much a matter of him getting to like the older missionaries and the nationals, but of making it possible for *them* to like *him*. In this respect I would like to give testimony that such new missionaries indeed often bring a fresh wind into a stuffy and even contaminated atmosphere. They often come with such a genuine and contagious radiance that they cannot but be a challenge to those who have lost the vision they had because of the exhaustion and the humdrum of every day. I think of Florence Allshorn, one of the missionary saints of the twentieth century. When she arrived on a mission station as a junior worker she was told to share a room with a cantankerous older woman with whom nobody managed to get along. She had, in fact, already been the cause of several resignations. When Florence entered the room, she found all the furniture and other possessions of the older lady arranged in one half of the room. Between that half and the other a clear straight chalk line was drawn on the floor, from wall to wall. And the very first words Florence heard from her new colleague were: "This is *my* half of the room; there is yours!" I bet none of us has ever had that kind of reception! Yet, because of the radiance of her truly Christian personality, Florence

was gradually able to penetrate the protective shield that
unlucky woman had built up all around herself over
many years. Patience, loving, and caring achieved what
nothing else could achieve. After that, the two of them
lived and worked together for a long time in true
harmony.

Something that has often struck and amazed me is that
some missionaries succeed in attracting gossip much
more easily than others. I have never been able to establish whether or not they actually encourage gossip,
but I do know that persons who persistently indicated
that they were not interested in gossip soon ceased to be
the confidants of the gossipers. Most gossiping is done so
subtly that it is difficult to detect. A newcomer may, for
instance, be influenced against a senior colleague by
means of vague insinuations. Without even realizing it,
he slowly becomes prejudiced against that person. Soon
he has a firm opinion of everyone he is living and working with, the result of having regularly received small
doses of sugarcoated malice.

Even our prayers may serve to subtly discredit our
colleagues. This is especially the case where two or three
choose to pray together regularly to the exclusion of
others because they "can pray over things more freely
where where there are only a few of us." Mildred Cable
and Francesca French, in their helpful booklet, *Ambassadors for Christ,* say that such people, "with all their
piety, instead of being spiritual rocks, become treach-
erous creeks where many a good reputation is lost in the
quicksand of confidential indiscretions. Under the excuse
of praying more freely where only a few meet, the law of
Christ which requires that one first speak to one's brother
alone is broken and the law of loyalty . . . violated."[18]

An additional problem lies in our readiness to prefer believing something bad rather than the good. This preference becomes the main source of the many small misunderstandings which abound in missionary communities. We catch only a fraction of a sentence here, we misinterpret a word or two there, and the damage is done. It appears to be extremely hard to accept that the overwhelming majority of people do indeed mean well, however unlikely this may appear to us!

All these diverse manifestations of self-assertion are, strange as it may sound, often nothing but signs of an inability to really accept oneself. It has frequently struck me that people who are, to a greater of lesser degree, misfits in their home environment, "square pegs in round holes," sometimes offer themselves for missionary service. Maybe such a person experiences some tension in his or her home environment or has a low level of adaptability. And now such a person comes to the conviction that God calls him or her to be a missionary. The subconscious idea seems to be that in the mission field, I will feel at home. After all, I will be working together with "dear children of the Lord" only.

Or take another example: somebody struggles with a secret or unconquered sin in his or her life, or a temptation that returns time and again. Everything he or she has tried to overcome that has been of no avail. And this person comes to the conviction that—if only I can live and work in an ideal environment I will surely conquer this problem. And, of course, the mission field would definitely be such an environment. Not only will I be surrounded and supported by dedicated colleagues, I will also prove to God that I am prepared to make an extraordinary sacrifice in leaving my home and country.

Without a doubt God will then give me the strength to overcome my weakness.

Of course it does not work out that way. On the contrary, the first person is on the mission field even more of a square peg in a round hole than was the case at home and the second soon discovers that his weakness has accompanied him and has actually increased.

These two examples are only two of the false surrenders to which missionaries are especially prone. It can take many other forms. Some missionaries try their best to let themselves disappear almost completely. They deliberately choose the most boring and exhausting jobs and set themselves impossible timetables with no opportunity for rest. They make unasked-for sacrifices for others which cause embarrassment and resentment rather than gratitude.

If all this was done in a spirit of true self-denial, it would be wonderful. One has the suspicion, however, that the opposite is often the case, in spite of what such missionaries may be saying. They would deny vehemently that they are, in reality, craving for recognition, and there is nothing they secretly long for more than that these sacrifices be acknowledged.

On close inspection this self-denial is really a form of sheer self-indulgence. Few things are as enjoyable as being miserable, especially if it is self-inflicted. It leads to a number of things. First, it gives cause for smugness. I once met a new missionary who told me, within ten minutes of our meeting, that he had earned a salary twice his present one in a congregation in his home country, but he had given it up to go to the mission field. Understandably, he did not last very long. He was too much aware of his sacrifices.

Second, self-inflicted misery tends to compromise others. Because of what I am doing for them, I make them dependent upon me. In this way I actually create greater room for myself in their lives while pretending that I do not expect anything in return.

Third, artificial martyrdom gives rise to the unshakable conviction that I am innocent when something goes wrong. "How on earth can it be my fault? I have not asked anything for myself, have I?"

The problem here is often not with people being prepared to sacrifice and to be the least, but with people insisting, however humbly, that they choose their own line of sacrifice.

Another form of false surrender is to refuse to enjoy anything. One reason for this refusal is the subconscious realization that, in order to truly enjoy I must be prepared to give myself to others. But to give myself in a genuine way implies becoming exposed and vulnerable, again implying the possibility of disappointment and pain. Many people cannot enjoy because they are incapable of dealing with disappointment. The person who can enjoy genuinely can also suffer genuinely. And, of course, if we are incapable of suffering we are also incapable of loving. So we flee from all this. And not infrequently the sources of our psychological problems lie just here.

A root problem of all this is to be found in the inability of people to accept themselves. We often emphasize self-denial as a prerequisite for missionary service, and that is correct, but we should never forget that true self-denial presupposes self-acceptance. Only persons who have found themselves can give themselves; otherwise, there is nothing to give. Missionaries, like other people, often have a natural resistance against being honest with themselves and giving true surrender.

Our inability to accept ourselves as we are reveals itself in many ways. It is, for instance, much easier to admit our own weakness than to admit our own insignificance. Often self-inflicted martyrdom is a means of covering up this nagging fear of being unimportant. It shows itself in our fear of making mistakes and the even greater fear of admitting mistakes. It also shows itself in the hesitation of some to speak the language of the people among whom they are working. I might make grammatical mistakes and people might laugh at me behind my back! The problem here is—to put it differently—my inability to distinguish between myself and my accomplishments. Instead of regarding my mistakes as my best, most faithful, and also most honest counselors I experience them as nothing but defeat.

Because of this fear we use masks. In fact, not a single one of us is really completely without a mask. We are all, to a greater or lesser extent, actors, pretending to be different from what we really are. A little boy said to his mother, "Why can't you be at home the way you are among other people?" You see, when there are visitors, Mother puts on her mask. She is friendly and courteous in the extreme. But the moment the visitors leave she takes off her mask and becomes her real self again.

To hide behind masks is something as old as humanity itself. Adam and Eve hid themselves behind fig leaves: they wore the first masks. "Am I my brother's keeper?" is the mask behind which Cain hid. Jacob came in Esau's garments, using Esau's name—a masked man, in order to receive his father's blessing. In reality, however, he received that blessing only twenty years later, and to

receive it had to be stripped of his mask. At the River
Jabbok a Man asked him, as did his father twenty years
before, "What is your name?" This time he had to speak
the truth, he had to take off his mask and admit, "I am
not Esau, but Jacob, the impostor!" Only after he had
taken off his mask could he receive his blessing and with
it a new name: Israel (Genesis 32:28).

Most of us have become so accustomed to our masks
that we are not even aware of them anymore. They fit so
comfortably! We slip them on mechanically when we go
out to attend to our various responsibilities. More or less
automatically we switch to what we have been trained to
do, concentrating on the shortcomings and needs of
others, be these spiritual or physical. We are the ones
who know, who have the answers and the remedies.
People look to us to show the way—at least this is what
we believe. And then we are surprised when we begin to
realize that we have not been able to get through to
them. Is it not, perhaps, because of the masks we wear?

In a very illuminating article Jacob Loewen tells a
moving story of what may happen when people indeed
take off their masks. He had accompanied a group of
students to a jail. They realized that it would serve little
purpose to preach about the sins of those behind the
bars. It is, after all, well known that prisoners almost always automatically parade their innocence; in other
words, they, too, hide behind masks. So the decision was
made to speak about the sins of those outside the bars
rather than those inside. "A college sophomore with a
radiant smile had been asked to give her testimony,"
Loewen reports. "When she got up in front of the jail
group, she grasped the bars with both hands and with a
voice choked with deep emotion revealed to the prisoners

that her father, a prominent minister, had committed suicide and that this had caused some very intense conflicts in her life. She admitted that in her darker moments she hated her father for what he had done to her reputation. Then again she realized in those very thoughts the depravity of her own heart and could only say that she was deeply grateful that she knew that God still cared for her, was concerned about her, and wanted her to find peace, joy, and meaning in life."

Now this was a testimony different from any other the prisoners had ever heard. In all other testimonies the emphasis had always been, "Let me tell you how bad I was. But now that I am a Christian, everything is completely different. I invite you all to become like me!" This kind of testimony would have had no effect on the prisoners. They would have recognized the mask. But that girl's disarming honesty was too much for them. One of them said, "I don't know why that girl had to be so honest. . . . She had no business taking off her mask like that. She wasn't that bad; not as bad as I am."[19]

In 2 Corinthians we see a similar spirit. Paul shows us that true surrender is to be found on the narrow road between self-assertion and false self-denial. He had the courage to be small and insignificant, and yet at the same moment that one has that courage, one ceases to be small and insignificant! Paul could admit that he had begged the Lord three times to rid him of his weakness but that his request was refused. Moreover, when accused and attacked by his opponents he made no attempt to justify himself in the same vein as the attack of the opponents, but acknowledged that they were perfectly right in what they said. He avoided all comparisons. When they argued that his weakness was real proof that he should be disqualified as an apostle, he took his joy and pride in the very things that were his weakness (12:9).

We will return, in the last chapter, to the way Paul boasted about his weakness. Here we refer to his boast only to show that he was prepared to take off his mask and also to walk the path of true surrender. His pride in weakness was not a form of self-inflicted martyrdom, nor an attempt to destroy himself. That would have been a sign of neurosis rather than self-denial. Although admitting the accusations of the opponents, from their point of view, he refused to allow them to trample upon him. He realized that more than just the man Paul was involved; the gospel itself was at stake. But that gospel could not be treated as though it could be neatly insulated from the person of the apostle. He was himself part of the message he proclaimed. He realized that he was but a "pot of earthenware" which contained the treasure of the gospel, but he also knew that the "transcendent power" of the gospel could be communicated only in this way (4:7).

It was for this reason that he wrote explicitly in 6:3, "In order that our service may not be brought into discredit, we avoid giving offence in anything." The missionary himself has to have credibility if the gospel is to have credibility; otherwise, he becomes a stumbling-block. The emphasis in this verse is on the "in anything." Paul therefore made great demands on himself. He realized the danger involved if he did not do that, for only a few sentences earlier he mentioned the terrible possibility of the Corinthians having received the grace of God in vain (6:1), because of his having failed to reveal the power of God's grace in his life. He had already written to the Corinthians in a similar vein in his first letter: "I bruise my own body and bring it into subjection, for fear that after preaching to others I should find myself rejected" (1 Corinthians 9:27).

The true missionary knows that, in one way or the other, Christ Himself has to become visible in his life and conduct. He resembles a movie screen onto which a live image is projected from a cubicle inside which is the invisible projector. In the same way, Christ Himself remains invisible in the background but out of the unseen His image is projected onto us missionaries and into us, taking shape in us and becoming visible until others recognize not us, but Christ in us. We are being transformed into His likeness, without even being aware of it. Perhaps this was Paul's message in that difficult passage in 2 Corinthians 3:18, "And because for us there is no veil over the face, we all reflect as in a mirror the splendor of the Lord; thus we are transfigured into his likeness, from splendor to splendor; such is the influence of the Lord who is Spirit."

It is the same idea Beatrice Cleland has expressed in a poem:

> Not merely by the words you say,
> Not only in your deeds confessed
> But in the most unconscious way
> Is Christ expressed.
>
> Is it a beatific smile?
> A holy light upon your brow?
> Oh, no—I felt His presence while
> You laughed just now.
>
> For me 'twas not the truth you taught,
> To you so clear, to me still dim,
> But when you came to me you brought
> A sense of Him.

And from your eyes He beckons me
And from your heart His love is shed,
Till I lose sight of you, and see
The Christ instead.

4

Your Servants for Christ's Sake

(2 Corinthians 3:1-3; 7:2-16)

In the previous chapter we looked at missionary spirituality primarily within the context of the missionary's personality and his being himself a part of the message he transmits. In the present chapter we want to continue more or less along the same lines, but with an emphasis rather on the missionary's relationship with nationals and with the national church.

I believe that the church discovers her true nature only as she moves from one human world to another, when she crosses frontiers, whether these are geographical, cultural, ethnic, linguistic, or sociological. The same discovery applies to the individual believer, especially the missionary, who is preeminently a person who crosses most of these frontiers. Of course there are missionaries who remain the same as they were before they left home, just as surely as there are many people who have never been missionaries in the traditional sense of the word and have never physically left their home environment but who have nevertheless crossed more frontiers than many missionaries did. The chances are, however, that the missionary would rather be the person who experiences the wonderful adventure of enrichment and renewal because of the many frontiers he or she crosses.

The Roman Catholic theologian, Ivan Illich, has defined missiology in a remarkable way:

> Missiology studies the growth of the Church into new peoples, the birth of the Church beyond its social boundaries; beyond the linguistic barriers within which she feels at home; beyond the poetical images in which she taught her children. The Church is led to marvel about the ever new images in which her venerable knowledge can become meaningful for the first time . . . missiology therefore is the study of the Church as surprise.[20]

I believe that all this becomes abundantly clear in the personality and ministry of Paul. There is something of the element of surprise in his ministry. Let us not for one moment assume that he had his "missionary theology" all made up and ready immediately after his conversion on the Damascus road. In fact, he did not even have it cut and dried when he was traversing Asia Minor with the gospel twenty years later. It was only gradually, as he moved from surprise to surprise, that he came to realize what the gospel really was. And the influence of his Gentile converts not only on his theological development but also on his spirituality was undoubtedly significant. For example, take his attitude toward the Jewish law. I would not have been surprised if, in the early years of his Christian life, Paul still thought it possible to reconcile his faith in Jesus Christ with the Jewish understanding of the law. He probably was, during the early stages, not so far removed from the Judaizers as we might think. Very much must have happened before he was able to say about his attitude to the law, his Jewish descent, and his membership of the party of the Pharisees, "All such assets I have written off because of Christ ... I count everything sheer loss. .... I count it so much garbage, for the sake of gaining Christ" (Philippians 3:7-9).

Much has been written about the differences between Paul and Peter as well as between Paul and James. I would like to submit that at least some of those differences in emphasis were due to the fact that Paul crossed the frontiers between Jews and Gentiles, whereas Peter and James remained essentially within the confines of Judaism.

When the Spirit sent Paul to the Greeks, it was not only to evangelize them; it was also to make it possible for Paul himself to see the real heart of his message:[21] Does not the same apply to today's missionary? Is it not true that the Spirit reveals to us many new things through the mediation of Christians in other cultures and contexts?

I would like to say again: what amazes me is to meet, over and over again, missionaries who have spent a lifetime in another culture but who have remained essentially the same persons they were when they first went there. Some of them are even more the same than they were before they went!

I am sure that this problem is not just one that touches upon the issue of effective communication of the gospel. It also touches upon the whole area of missionary spirituality. And the reason for this state of affairs lies, I believe in the inability of many Westerners to really see and accept other races as people.

You might raise an eyebrow here and say,"The writer comes from South Africa where whites indeed do not regard blacks as human beings. That is why he has this bee in his bonnet. This problem does not exist elsewhere anymore, at any rate not among our missionaries." I wish I could be sure that this is really so. I fear, however, that our Western feelings of superiority are so deep-seated that they usually remain in one form or another, even where we have taken all possible care to suppress them.

In the first chapter I referred to research done by Gordon Frazer into the reasons for first-term failures among American missionaries. One of the twelve categories in his list was: "Inability to suppress a feeling of superiority to nationals or national workers." This item was responsible for 13 percent of all the casualties—the third highest on the list of twelve! Once again you might say, Yes, but that survey was done more than a decade ago! My counter-question would be: Are we sure that it is so much different today, or have we just learned to cover up our superiority feelings a bit better? It may help us if we realize that this feeling of superiority may manifest itself in a thousand subtle ways. It is to be found when missionaries act as though the national church is there for their sake, not the other way around. It is also to be detected where we keep on giving and doing, thus expressing our love in a one-way movement only, from us to them. It is still the same problem that presents itself when national Christians say of a missionary, "He loves us only in the Lord!" or when a national bishop remarks of a highly intelligent and able missionary, about to leave on furlough, "What a pity! He's learned nothing while he's been with us. He always knew."

Some missionaries have naively thought that they could solve the problem simply by renouncing their origins. An American missionary to a country in Africa used to say, "I always try to forget I am an American." That's fine, but do the Africans forget? Of course they don't. So the missionary from the West is burdened with the image of his race, even if he himself has succeeded in overcoming all imaginable barriers. For example, a friend, a white missionary of the Dutch Reformed Church, once wrote a letter to a black medical student. This student was the son of a black minister in the Dutch Reformed Church and the missionary knew him from sight. He had heard, however, that the young black man was experiencing various problems and frustrations. So, to encourage him, he wrote him a letter. After about two months he received a reply, which ran as follows:

Dear Rev.,
Let me say at this stage that I did receive your letter, but due to extreme pressure of work I couldn't answer. Anyhow, that's part of the truth—the other part being that I haven't yet worked out what kind of relationship I'm to have with white Dutch Reformed Church ministers since most of those working with my father are usually arrogant, rude, and condescending. Your surname happens to be Afrikaans; that just about condemns you.

I'm being very candid, so much so that it sounds rude but let me assure you at this stage it's not my intention to be rude.

I'm also told by my parents that I owe you a letter which indeed I do but every time I set out to write (including this time) I couldn't for the life of me think what we'd talk about. . . .

For some reason or other I couldn't ask my father this, but could you tell me how black people are to relate to and identify with the Dutch Reformed Church? Not on an emotional level—but on a . . . logical and intellectual level?

Hope you are still well.
Yours faithfully,
N.N.

This extreme example may help to open our eyes to the many less conspicuous instances when we are just not allowed to forget that we are Westeners and have to carry this burden along with us. I would like to add, though, that it is not only impossible to forget our origins but also unnecessary and wrong. Paul, in spite of what he wrote to the Philippians, never ceased being a Jew. Indeed, it is only when we are rooted in our own origins that we can also meaningfully relate to other peoples. A French Roman Catholic missionary to Tanzania, B. Joinet, has written movingly on this in an article significantly entitled "I Am a Stranger in My Father's House." It has been translated into a number of languages and re-printed in many magazines. A few years later he supplemented it with another article, "I Speak in the House of My Hosts."[22] In both these papers Joinet reveals an unusual degree of perceptivity regarding this whole problem of the relationship between the missionary and the national church. Something that comes out forcefully in both titles as well as in the articles themselves is that I can only hope to be a true stranger or guest as long as I remain a native of my own land. I can err in two ways, either by remaining so aloof that it is impossible to identify with the young church or by foisting myself on them by playing national.

What can be discovered in this respect, in Paul's second letter to the Corinthians? Of course, Paul did not have the problems we have as a result of the legacy of the colonial era, but Jew-Gentile relationships were the cause of major problems. In fact, even if Paul had been a Greek but not a Corinthian, he would have experienced some tensions. So we do not see Paul foisting himself upon the Corinthians, as though he were one of them, barging in through closed doors, forgetting that he was a stranger and guest. Neither do we see him keeping aloof, addressing them from a great distance, always remaining the outsider.

One of the most striking images he uses to describe the relationship between himself and the Corinthian Church is to refer to them as "a letter that has come from Christ" (cf. 3:1-3). Paul's opponents have arrived in Corinth with glowing letters of recommendation from elsewhere. Paul himself does not need any such letters or paper credentials, for the Church in Corinth is his letter of recommendation.

The way this letter has come into existence is described in a remarkable way. Paul does not claim that he has written this letter, as we missionaries tend to be doing ("I founded a church here, or established a congregation there.") No, the Author of this letter is Christ, and He has written it with the Spirit of the living God. Paul is the ambassador who has had to deliver the letter, or, as it says in the Greek, the letter "has been ministered by us" or "prepared through our service" (10:3). Everybody, Paul says, can see the letter for what it is and read it for himself. It gives testimony primarily to its Author, but undoubtedly also to His ambassador.

Furthermore, Paul calls himself the *servant* of the

Church in Corinth, for Christ's sake (4:5). As a matter of fact, the word "servant" and its related forms occupy a key place in this letter. Paul refers to himself and his fellow workers as "servants of a new covenant" (3:6) and as "God's servants" (6:4). He refers to the "ministry of the Spirit" (3:8), the "ministry of righteousness" (3:9) and the "ministry of reconciliation" (5:18).

Today often a tension exists between being servant of God and being servant of the church, between ministering to God and ministering to man. In recent theological discussions there has often been a tendency to see these as mutually exclusive: the church is either the church for God or the church for others. Paul would have been genuinely surprised to hear of such theological developments. To be the church for others is to be the church for Christ, and vice versa (cf. 2 Corinthians 2:14-16; 3:3; 4:5; 5:13; 12:15, 19). Living for Christ is, in the concretization of the encounter, living for others and serving them.[23] God and man, as was already noted, are not and should never be competitors for our love.

In this spirit of the gospel Paul approaches the church in Corinth. He could have laid claim to their loyalty on the basis of the authority of his apostolate, but he declines to do that. He is prepared to take the risk of being rejected. He creates enough room for them to say no to him. He opts for vulnerability. He finds the delicate balance Joinet has talked about, being in his Father's house where he presumably has certain rights, yet nevertheless being a stranger in that house, without rights or claims.

Our problem as missionaries often lies in the fact that we want to be servants of the younger church, but that we want to be servants in our way. All missionaries, says

Joinet, like to say, with John the Baptist: "He must increase, but I must decrease" (John 3:30), and it is easy to say that during a retreat. But, in actual practice, who wants to decrease? This is especially difficult if we are absolutely convinced that we know better, if we daily see new proofs of the fact that things in the younger church are heading for disaster, so that we had better intervene as quickly as possible.

I am not suggesting that we should not intervene at all. I do believe, however, that there are more ways than one in which this could be done. We could see ourselves, to use another metaphor of Joinet, either as chauffeur or as spare wheel. The chauffeur takes over the whole show and steers in the direction he has chosen, but the spare wheel's role is complementary. A spare wheel is very important, though, especially if the nearest service station happens to be 200 miles away. Paul in this letter to the Corinthians is more spare wheel than chauffeur. At no point does he offer—let alone demand—to take over the steering wheel. Throughout he does exactly what a good spare wheel is supposed to do: he assures the Corinthians that he is there, at their disposal, should they need him. He gives them reassurance because they know that he is there if they need him. He makes himself available. He has no desire that the Corinthians should "blow a tire," which would compel him to leave everything else and rush off to them. In fact, he tries everything in his power to prevent the possibility of a tire being blown. For this reason he nurses the church as gently and lovingly as possible.

Especially in the seventh chapter this nurture becomes apparent. He puts the Corinthian automobile through a road test and by and large he finds it to be quite road worthy. "I have great pride in you," he says (v. 4). The arrival of Titus has put his mind at ease even more: "He has told us how you long for me, how sorry you are and how eager to take my side; and that has made me happier still" (v. 7). He regrets the pain his previous letter had caused them, but is at the same time grateful "that the wound has led to a change of heart" (v. 9). "You bore your hurt in God's way, and see what its results have been! . . . At every point you have cleared yourselves of blame" (v. 11). Not only is Paul himself greatly encouraged; he has "also been delighted beyond everything by seeing how happy Titus is; you have all helped to set his mind completely at rest" (v. 13). All along Paul has boasted to Titus about the Corinthians; now he is glad that the "proud boast" he has made in the presence of Titus "has proved true" (v. 14). And so Paul concludes the passage jubilantly, "How happy I am now to have complete confidence in you!" (v. 16).

So his anxiety does not concern the Corinthians as such. What he fears is that other chauffeurs may come along and highjack the Corinthian church. It is to warn them against this that he offers his service. What strikes us once again is the delicate tension between intimate involvement and identification on the one hand and standing back just a little bit on the other. So Paul never compromises the Corinthians up to their very necks; neither does he in any way suggest abandoning them.

Missionaries find themselves in the same dilemma today. Because of our history of paternalism and racial superiority feelings, we are usually in little danger of identifying too closely with people in the younger churches. We so easily see our responsibility as disposed of when we have imparted the gospel to a people, established a younger church with its own indigenous ministry, and taught them some Western administrative machinery. In all this the emphasis is almost entirely on one-way communication. We tell them exactly how they ought to behave, what they ought to do, how they ought to believe, and what they ought to abandon. We prescribe carefully prepared gospel recipes. But—and this is the core of the problem—only rarely do we allow them to *experience* all this together with us. They do not go with us on a journey of discovery to search and find together. They are simply being provided with the net result of do this, believe as follows, leave that! They get the ready answer but have not struggled with us in trying to solve the problem.

In the previous chapter we have put the finger on one of the basic causes for our predilection for such a one-way traffic. We hate to expose ourselves, to take off our masks, for we do not want them to peep into our own struggles and weaknesses, into our own processes of spiritual development. We present ourselves to them as those who already have all the answers, who are finished products, and who have now come to tell them what to do to become like us. We are doctors handing out prescriptions to patients for diseases which do not trouble us in the least.

The result, more often than not, is that we train parrots instead of building up people. The Christians in the younger churches learn to make the same noises we make and if we hear these we fool ourselves into believing that our mission work has been successful. When we hear them preach, pray, or witness, we say: "How beautiful! Our work has been blessed tremendously!" A Scottish missionary to Zambia relates his experience in the younger church in that country: "On our first coming into the church here, we were deeply impressed by its evangelical character, and the strength of its evangelical preaching. ... And then we found that the preaching is almost entirely the recital of set formulae learned from our predecessors, bearing almost no relation to the everyday life of the people, either Christian or non-Christian."[24] The young Christians have merely repeated the right words after the missionaries, but have never internalized the message because they were not given the opportunity to make the discovery of what it means to be Christians together with them. Because of this, much of the indigenous Christianity may be shallow and disappointments, as we call them, sometimes come from those Christians with the most pious testimonies. "Inexplicably," we would say, such a Christian has committed a shocking sin, and we throw our arms up in horror.

The question is where ought we to look for what has gone wrong? Are they to blame, or are *we*? To put it differently: if we, for the sake of argument, may be so arrogant as to accept that we are spiritually more advanced and stable than many national Christians, to what do we attribute this? How have we come where we are? Was it through one-way spiritual traffic directed at us? No, we know that this was not the case. We got where we are through intimate experiences of faith together with others, through participating with others in our search for light and growth, through discussing and praying and often agonizing with other Christians.

One asks, then, whether we will be able to transmit these intimate experiences of the love and grace of God to other people in any other way than by walking this road with them. I sincerely doubt it. We may produce

puppets who react when we pull the strings, but we will
not experience the joy of helping to form mature Christians.

In many African languages there is a proverb which in
Zulu is *Umuntu ngumuntu ngabantu.* Translated
literally it says: "Man is a man through men." In other
words, "No man is an island; he only becomes man
through his fellowmen." There is profound wisdom in
this proverb. By participating in the other man's humanity we are both shaped and led to maturity. This is
preeminently true of the black man in Africa. For
example, I have often noticed that, after a service, the
black Christians do not at all appear eager to return to
their homes. They linger awhile, almost as though they
are unsatisfied, as though they are waiting for more or for
something else. The religious service with its emphasis
on preaching and one-way communication has not been
enough. There still remains the desire to share, to
experience fellowship, to reach out to one another. Is this
not an indictment against us that we have failed in love
and identification with them?

We usually know exactly what we have gone to give to
people in Third World countries: the faith, salvation,
education, health services, technological development,
social progress. We do not know as clearly what we have
gone to receive. We often go as a rich uncle who pays a
visit to poor relatives and hands out chocolates and
pocket money to his nephews and nieces. Some years ago
Orlando Costas spoke at Fuller Theological Seminary on
"Mission Out of Affluence."[25] Affluence here means
more than just being rich in the literal sense of the word.
It stands for a whole mentality of being independent of
others, of being able to go it alone and disregard others,

of having to spare. And deep down in our hearts we Westerners believe we have to spare, not only financially but also technically and spiritually. Out of our abundance we give money, manpower, know-how, and faith. It costs us little, because we can do without that which we have extra.

This attitude and the complementary image of the rich uncle have devastating consequences in our missionary work. Daniel T. Niles, the well-known church leader from Sri Lanka, suggested another image—the beggar. The missionary, he said, is a beggar telling other beggars where they would find bread. We are all beggars, then, the difference being that we know where to go for food and the others don't. But we are as dependent as they are on the bread. And we have to share it with them. As a matter of fact, it is only as we share it with them that we become fully aware of its true taste and nutritious value. So, in our mission work, we are not only dependent on that bread but also on those who share it with us. True love is not just to be giving ourselves to others, because, as Joinet points out, this may lead to them feeling inferior. The relationship between missionaries and nationals has far too often been that of condescending benefactors and irritated recipients of charity. True love, on the other hand, is accepting that you are dependent and expecting something from the other one. This attitude helps one to discover himself and also to discover avenues of giving. The best I can give somebody is to enable him to become a giver. Is that not what Paul says in Ephesians 4:16: "Christ . . . is the head, and on him the whole body depends. Bonded and knit together by every constituent joint, the whole frame grows through the due activity of each part, and builds itself up in love."

There is an important side effect to this reciprocity in giving which is difficult to express. If we are mutually dependent on one another, we develop the boldness not only to give to one another but also to make demands on one another. We become, to one another, open doors in lieu of doors which have remained shut. For example, one day a venerable black Methodist pastor in Johannesburg walked into the office of a white friend, grabbed the white man by the collar, and shook him violently while at the same time pouring a torrent of accusations on him and all white people for what they were doing to blacks. The white man was completely taken by surprise and it took him quite a while to realize what was happening. The black man had just had another humiliating experience with a white official somewhere in the city, but he could not show how he felt about that. So all his pent-up fury was let loose on one of the few white men he really trusted. What he did that day was, in fact, an expression of confidence, a proof of mutual acceptance and dependence.

One evening, during the Lausanne Congress on World Evangelization (1974), it happened that I, another white South African, five or six black South Africans, and two American Mennonites had our evening meal together. We started talking and after the evening meal, instead of going to the plenary session, we just continued talking as a group and soon a pattern developed. The blacks were relating humorous anecdotes about their encounters with South Africa's apartheid society. There was no end to the stories they were telling, some of which were hilariously funny. I remember one of the group, an elderly black Anglican bishop, being almost incapable of proceeding with his anecdotes because of being totally overcome with laughter. I gradually realized what was taking place. We know, of course, that fun and laughter are very close to sorrow and that they may actually serve to help us digest the sorrow. Humor has a therapeutic value. But I think there was more than that. We four white men—two South Africans and two Americans—were *needed* that evening as symbols of the very thing those blacks were joking about and rebelling against. But their being able to do what they did in our company was also a vote of confidence and a sign of acceptance and mutual interdependence. In effect, they were saying, that we need one another.

Perhaps these two very down-to-earth examples can show us what is at stake here. Being dependent on one another usually does not manifest itself in the spectacular and the dramatic, but much rather in the ordinary encounters and events of every day.

There is something else to this. If we remain at a safe distance, there is a real danger of us becoming callous and insensitive in the face of the squalor and misery so many people in the Third World are suffering. There is also an opposite danger of being completely suffocated and burdened beyond endurance by the awareness of guilt feelings because we are unable to alleviate the distress of these people. Many missionaries feel the poverty, squalor, evil, and sin of others so acutely that both their sanity and their faith are endangered. In other cases this leads to over-compensation which frequently manifests itself in new forms of paternalism and condescension.

The answer lies, once again, not in the right balance between callousness and oversensitivity, but rather in giving ourselves wholeheartedly, as if everything depends on us, while at the same time casting all our concerns on the Lord as if everything depends on Him. We should neither attempt to rationalize away all our responsibility and involvement nor allow ourselves to be so crushed by the unbearable burden of what we think we ought to do but cannot accomplish. Our good works are a sign and a proof of our faith, but it is ultimately by faith, not by all our good works, that we are justified. We may therefore indeed cast all our weaknesses and even our failures on the Lord.

5

The Courage to Be Weak

(2 Corinthians 4:1-18; 5:11-17; 6:1-10; 12:6-10)

In Paul's second letter to the Corinthians a number of key concepts recur surprisingly often and with which the apostle characterizes his ministry and himself. The most important ones are: weakness (ἀσθένεια), ministry or service (διακονία), suffering (λύπη), and affliction (θλίψις). They are all, in one way or another, synonyms. But then there are some other key concepts set off against those and used equally frequently by Paul in this letter—concepts such as power (δύναμς), joy (χαρά), and boasting (καύχησις). Only the letter to the Philippians has more references to joy than this one, whereas boasting and its related forms occur more times in 2 Corinthians than in Romans, Galatians, Philippians, and 1 Corinthians taken together.

In this last chapter I intend to take a closer look at these two seemingly contradicting sets of concepts, ask-

ing ourselves what bearing they have on missionary spirituality.

No one has emphasized the weakness and the fragility
of the missionary as clearly as Paul did in this letter.[26]
Nowhere has the disproportion between the magnitude
of the missionary's task and goal and the flimsiness of his
equipment been underlined more clearly. True mission is
the weakest and least impressive human activity
imaginable, the very antithesis of a theology of glory.

The important point to recognize here is that all this is
so, not by accident but by definition. It is a necessary
precondition for any authentic mission. In this Paul
follows his Master. José Comblin stated it well: "He
(Jesus) did not try to impress (people) with power. The
typical messianism of his day was quite alien to him, and
the supreme sign he gave to people was his own death. It
was a visible manifestation of his complete inability to
convince and dominate people by arguments based on
the trappings of human cultures and human civiliza-
tions."[27] Jesus was no Messiah in the popular sense, and
in the final analysis this was the reason for His cruci-
fixion.

The same issue of messianism was at stake in the controversy between Paul and his opponents in Corinth. He
brings this out in a remarkable way in 2 Corinthians 6:8-
10. We have here seven clauses, each of which is in-
troduced in Greek by (ὡς). This does not, in the
context, mean "as if." Paul is not suggesting that the
conditions he refers to here are not real; on the contrary,
they are very real. The (ὡς) is saying that it is normal
for Paul's apostleship to be carried on under these conditions: being unknown, dying, disciplined, in sorrow and
poverty are the true marks of an apostle.[28] Weakness is an

authentic characteristic of the apostolic ministry. Without the weakness which his opponents deride, there can be no real apostolic ministry and no true proclamation of Christ. The church is not made up of spiritual giants; only broken men can lead others to the cross. It is on men like Peter that Jesus builds His church.[29] The possibility of change and conversion is based on humans being vulnerable; it does not, however, involve the vulnerability only of the one whom we would like to convert but also our own vulnerability as missionaries. Jesus revealed what sin is only because He Himself had been vulnerable; had He opted for invulnerability the true nature of sin would have remained hidden.

When we realize that Christians are weak, we usually react in one of two ways. I use my weakness as an excuse or I reject it and demand strength. If I use weakness as an excuse I am not to blame for what is happening. God has caused me to be as weak as I am, therefore He is to be blamed if things go wrong. In fact, arguing this way, our weakness does not only become an excuse but a virtue. We are grateful for being weak because this relieves us of all responsibility; we may relax with a clear conscience.

The other human reaction is to reject the road of weakness and demand strength and power from God. Once the disciples of Jesus arrived at a Samaritan village to make arrangements for Jesus and their friends to spend the night there. But, as Luke tells us, "The villagers would not have him because he was making for Jerusalem" (Luke 9:53). When James and John saw this they were furious and said to Jesus, "Lord, may we call down fire from heaven to burn them up?" (v. 54). They were unable to accept weakness as a true concomitant to discipleship. "Lord, give us strength, power!" they said.

Paul had a similar problem of which he tells us in 2 Corinthians 12. He takes his mask off and reveals his humanness. His readers can identify with him, for he does not try to put up a show. We do not know what the "thorn in the flesh" (v. 7) really was. But we do know that, for a long time, Paul was unable to reconcile himself to it. He regarded it as "Satan's messenger" who had come to bruise him. So he thought he had every reason to beg the Lord to rid him of it. After all, the Lord has promised us victory over Satan!

It took Paul a long time to realize what this was all about. And here, in chapter 12, he puts it into words. He has, at long last, discovered that he needed the thorn in the flesh, even if it were Satan's messenger! It would save him from being unduly elated (v. 7)! It would prevent him from falling into the same trap into which his opponents had fallen. So now he has reached the point where he can accept God's ruling: "My grace is all you need; power comes to its full strength in weakness" (v. 9).

I believe that every one of us needs and in fact has his or her own "thorn in the flesh." Some of us are possibly well aware of what it is, others not, or not quite clearly. I doubt whether we should now embark upon a frantic search to identify our various "thorns in the flesh." This could easily become such a form of masochism that we become so preoccupied with this "thorn" that our whole ministry becomes paralyzed. Unfortunately, this is exactly what happens to some missionaries.

Paul, on the contrary, lets the whole matter rest, not wasting more time on it. He has accepted God's ruling. More than that, he has turned this enormous liability into an asset! For we hear him saying, "I ... prefer to find my joy and pride in the very things that are my weakness" (v. 9). Instead of harassing God any further to remove the "thorn," he will boast about it.

This means a revaluation of all values, such as abound in the entire second epistle to the Corinthians. It is impostors who speak the truth, unknown men who are known to all. It is the dying who still live on and the sorrowful who always have cause for joy. It is the poor who bring wealth to many and the penniless who own the world (6:8-10). These are the inescapable paradoxes of the Christian faith. Just as, in Jesus, the paradox of heavenly glory and the cross coexist, the paradoxes of power and weakness and of life and death coexist in the ministry and faith of the apostle. This enables Paul to say to the Corinthians, "For when I am weak, then I am strong" (12:10), an expression which Ernst Fuchs rightly refers to as "the most famous paradox in the entire New Testament."[30] As Jesus died on the cross in weakness, yet now lives by the power of God, "we who share his weakness shall by the power of God live with him in your service" (13:4). Hence Paul is "well content, for Christ's sake, with weakness, contempt, persecution, hardship, and frustration" (12:10).

There remains, however, an element of restraint in his boasting. He has not himself chosen this road; he was forced by his opponents to take it. He therefore repeatedly says that such boasting is folly and that, if he takes part in the boasting competition, he does it as a fool (11:1, 16, 17, 21; 12:11). In 12:11 he says explicitly, "I am being very foolish, but it was you who drove me to it; my credentials should have come from you." So he remains apologetic about it. In fact, one discerns especially in the first verses of chapter 12, a remarkable restraint. He talks about himself in the third person, "I know a Christian man who fourteen years ago ... was caught up as far as the third heaven. And I know that this same man ... was caught up into paradise. ... About such a man as that I am ready to boast; but I will not boast on my own account, except of my weaknesses" (12:2-5).

Another aspect of Paul's suffering already touched upon in a previous chapter, is worth noticing. In the letter to the Colossians Paul says that suffering is his way of helping to complete, in his poor human flesh, "the full tale of Christ's affliction still to be endured, for the sake of his body which is the church" (Colossians 1:24). Paul is not suggesting that Christ's sufferings were not adequate. He does say, however, that more sufferings will follow, for only in this way can the church be built up. And he sees his own sufferings as contributing to that. He therefore ascribes salvational value to his sufferings. Without them, the full tale of Christ's sufferings remains incomplete. His suffering is "for the sake of the gospel" (2 Timothy 1-8). To the Corinthians he therefore says: "If distress be our lot, it is the price we pay for your consolation, for your salvation" (2 Corinthians 1:6). And if he says, a few chapters further on, "Death is at work in us, and life in you" (4:12), he means the same thing. His suffering brings life to them. He is even prepared to go beyond the limit of the suffering he has already endured, if only this would be beneficial to the Corinthians. "As for me, I will gladly spend what I have for you—yes, and spend myself to the limit" (12:15).

The world of Paul is very different from our modern consumer society in which things are defined and evaluated—dividends, turnover, and success. I read the following on the jacket of a well-known book by a well-known Christian author: "Let Dr. X give you ten simple, workable goals for developing confidence; three proven secrets for keeping up your vigor; thirteen actual examples of how prayer power helped people in need; four words that lead to success; five actual techniques used by successful men to overcome defeat; an eight-point spiritual healing formula; a ten-point guide to popularity." The world of Paul's thinking is different from this approach. Apostolic ministry is always arduous and done in feebleness, a world where the blood of the martyrs is the seed of the church. That which his opponents reject is precisely what Paul chooses to be the center of his message and his life: weakness, affliction, and self-denial.

The difference between Paul and his opponents, we have said, lies in the cross. Apostolic theology, says Kosuke Koyama, must be stigmatized theology.[31] He compares the hands of the Crucified with those of Lenin and of the Buddha. If Jesus' hands were closed tight like Lenin's, theology would become ideology. If his hands were open, very much open, with symbolic webs between the fingers so as to be able to scoop up everybody, like the hands of the Buddha, theology would lose its quality of being a stumbling-block. But now his hands are neither open, nor closed; they are defenseless, and pierced through.

Often when we have differences among ourselves and argue about the essence of the gospel, those defenseless, beaten, and defeated hands are not in evidence. One muscular Christ confronts another similarly muscular one, resulting in the print of the nails disappearing behind the flexing of those powerful muscles. And if the other person's Christ becomes too muscular, I retreat into my shell. Moreover, the more muscular our Christ becomes, the more difficult it will be to rehabilitate him back to Calvary. The cross, we ought to remember, is the hallmark of the church. When the resurrected Christ appeared to His disciples, His *scars* were the proof of His identity. Because of them the disciples believed (John 20:20). Will it be different with us? Will the world believe unless they can recognize the marks of the cross on us?

On the basis of the centrality of the cross Paul's ministry is characterized by modesty. Such modesty does not, however, in any way exclude conviction, which is a difficult lesson for us missionaries to learn. We seem to think that modesty, nonaggression, being considerate and tolerant in our ministry imply a degree of haziness and even indulgence on our part. Conversely, if we believe that we can only proclaim the gospel on the basis of a clear conviction that it is the only saving message, we tend to go about in an arrogant and uncompromising way, even to the point of imposing ourselves and our message upon others.

In 2 Corinthians Paul shows us a third way. Although going about in a humble, modest, and unassuming way, he leaves no doubt about his conviction that the message he proclaims involves a matter of life and death. This conviction becomes clear in the passage where he likens himself and his fellow workers to "incense offered by Christ to God." He reveals the effect the fragrance of that incense has on those who are on the way to salvation, as well as on those who are on the way to perdition: "to the latter it is a deadly fume that kills, to the former a vital fragrance that brings life" (2:16). The apostolic ministry, however modest and weak, does not remain without effect. Nobody remains neutral; salvation itself is at stake here.

Paul can adopt this attitude in the light of the fact that the great eschatological turning point has already come. The *New English Bible,* which translates 5:16 as follows, "With us therefore worldly standards have ceased to count in our estimate of any man," fails to properly reflect three important Greek words: ἀπὸ τοῦ νῦν "from now on." Paul is saying that something has happened that makes everything different "from now on." He says it more explicitly in 6:2, where he quotes from Isaiah 49:8, "In the hour of my favour I gave heed to you; on the day of deliverance I came to your aid." The prophet used those words within the context of a prophecy about the distant future, but Paul applies it to his own time, for he adds directly, "The hour of favour has now come; now, I say, has the day of deliverance dawned."

This emphasis shows that Paul has grasped the significance of the coming of Jesus and of Jesus' own understanding of His coming. When the Nazarene appeared on the scene, the various Jewish religious groups either had a one-sided interest in the remote past which was glorified out of all proportions, or they had an exaggerated interest in the future, which would actually mean a return to the glorious past. Moreover, both positions were often held by the same people. The present period in which they lived was, however, completely empty, void of any meaning, and abandoned to the dominion of evil and suffering. Jesus, however, evaluated the present differently. He caused a furor in Nazareth when He quoted from Isaiah and then continued: "Today, in your very hearing, this text has come true" (Luke

4:21). It was no longer necessary to expect the coming of the kingdom for the distant future only, for the kingdom had already come (Matthew 12:28; Luke 11:20), it was in the very midst of the people (Luke 17:21). To His disciples He said: "Happy the eyes that see what you are seeing! I tell you, many prophets and kings wished to see what you now see, yet never saw it; to hear what you now hear, yet never heard it!" (Luke 10:24).

In this connection we have to interpret the exceptionally pregant Greek concept Καιρός . It means: the decisive moment, the turning point in history. Jesus rebuked the Jewish leaders for their inability to recognize the Καιρός. "What hypocrites you are! You know how to interpret the appearance of earth and sky; how is it you cannot interpret this fateful hour?" (Luke 12:56). To the city of Jerusalem he said: "They will encircle you and hem you in at every point; they will bring you to the ground, you and your children within your walls, and not leave one stone standing on another, because you did not recognize God's moment when it came" (Luke 19:43,44).

The early church retained the consciousness of the fact that a radically new age was inaugurated by Jesus. Christ was raised from the dead, and the Spirit had descended upon the church. We have received the "first fruits" of the new age which has invaded the old and wounded it mortally. It is therefore by no means accidental that specifically in 2 Corinthians Paul refers to the Holy Spirit as ἀρραβών : "It is God who has set his seal upon us, and as a pledge of what is to come has given the Spirit to dwell in our hearts" (1:22; cf. 5:5).

The breaking in of the new age has tremendous consequences. "When anyone is united to Christ, there is a new world; the old order has gone, and a new order has already begun" (5:17). In the authentic apostolic ministry the εδχατον has become a present reality. It ceases to be merely a future reality toward which we are on the way; it has invaded and permeated our earthly historical existence and is in the process of transforming it. Because the decisive moment has arrived, the apostolic ministry is "a fragrance of life unto life" (2:16), through which a great splendor manifests itself in the divine dispensation of the Spirit (3:8), a splendor that brings people justification (3:9) and reconciliation (5:20).

The new creation is an indisputable reality for Paul. This knowledge does not cause him any euphoria, though, for he knows that the old order, although "already gone" (5:17) is still casting a dark and menacing shadow over everything. We do not yet experience the kingdom in its fullness. We still live in the unredeemed world, but we may walk with our heads held high; we know that the kingdom is coming because it has already come. We live within the creative tension between the already and the not yet, forever moving closer to the orbit of the former. We Christians are an anachronism in this world: not anymore what we used to be, but not yet what we are destined to be. We are too early for heaven, yet too late for the world. We live on the borderline between the already and the not yet. We are a fragment of the world to come, God's colony in a human world, his experimental garden on earth. We are like crocuses in the snow, a sign of the world to come and at the same time a guarantee of its coming.

It is particularly in the fourth chapter of 2 Corinthians that this life-in-paradox is apparent. We are like pots of earthenware containing a treasure, says Paul (v. 7). Therefore, in spite of being hard-pressed on every side, we are never hemmed in; though bewildered, we are never at our wits' end; though struck down, we are not left to die (vv. 8, 9). These statements don't suggest an attitude of obstinacy by the apostle, as though he is refusing to look obvious facts in the face, but a position of acting on the conviction that the decisive turn in history has already been accomplished.

He therefore moves in two worlds, for he says, in verse 10, that he is carrying death and life, at the same time, or, as he explains in the next verse, "While still alive, we are being surrendered into the hands of death, for Jesus' sake, so that the life of Jesus also may be revealed in this mortal body of ours." He has no fear of death, though, for he knows that God who has raised Jesus to life, will, "with Jesus, raise us too, and bring us to his presence" (v. 14).

In verse 16 he interrupts himself and says exuberantly, "No wonder we do not lose heart!" Indeed, for although "our outward humanity is in decay, yet day by day we are inwardly renewed. Our troubles are slight and short-lived; and their outcome an eternal glory which outweighs them far" (vv. 16, 17). It is the future that determines the present, the new age that determines the old, not the other way around.

Paul therefore uses very ordinary words in a different way from our tendency to use them. Such an ordinary word which occurs frequently in 2 Corinthians is "patience." Our use of it often contains an element of fatalism such as, "You have just got to be patient in spite of everything you see." Not so Paul. In his usage, the word "patience" has an element of expectancy in it and all ideas of fatalism are completely absent. The same is true of the word "hope." When we say, "Well, we just hope for the best," we are actually saying that all evidence is to the contrary. Hope in this sense is in fact a statement of despair. Christian hope does not spring from despair about the present time, however; it is based on that which is already a reality. It is both possession and yearning, repose and activity, arrival and journey. Hope is the connecting line between the already and the not yet, between the penultimate and the ultimate. We dream about the future by working to make it come true. As Paul says elsewhere, "I have not yet reached perfection, but I press on, hoping to take hold of that for which Christ once took hold of me" (Phil. 3:12). Authentic Christian hope is hope-in-the-process-of-fulfillment. It is for this reason that Paul can say: we were saved (past tense) in hope.

As with patience and hope, so joy is understood in a new way in the Pauline epistles. Joy, with us, is often a kind of natural disposition, an attribute of people who are by nature optimists. It is a mood or a state of mind. It is dependent upon circumstances. Paul, however—as already pointed out—uses χαρά, joy, more frequently in Philippians and in 2 Corinthians than anywhere else, and these are preeminently letters written against a background of sorrow and pain. "In all our many troubles my cup is full of consolation and overflows with joy" (2 Cor. 7:4). So the apostle's joy is no joy in spite of pain and affliction, as we might put it, but *in* sorrow and pain.[32]

We come to the end. I believe that Paul's existence on the borderline between the already and the not yet, in that reaching out for what lies ahead and pressing toward the goal (cf. Phil. 3:14), is of tremendous importance for our missionary existence today. It ought to be the very antithesis of neutral aloofness, contentment, and passivity, as it ought to be the antithesis of shallow enthusiasm and hyperactivity.

More important, because Paul lived in the creative tension we referred to, Paul never doubted that he was where he belonged and was doing what he should be doing. The gnawing uncertainity about whether or not we should continue more than anything else hollows out our ministry and destroys our joy.

It is as true of the modern missionary, as it has always been of all the generations of missionaries since Paul, that we will not be able to cope with frustrations, disappointments, disillusionment, and shock unless we know that we belong where we are, and are able to draw courage from that knowledge. In Troas Paul had a vision of a Macedonian appealing to him and saying, "Come across to Macedonia and help us" (Acts 16:10). Yet upon arrival in Philippi, no county orchestra or reception committee greeted him, rather a whip, and a cell in the local prison. Yet he persevered, with joy, for he knew: "This is where I belong!"

The same is true through all the centuries of the Christian church. The Ugandan church recently had its centennial. Just over a hundred years ago eight missionaries left England and went there, and in less than two years' time only one was left alive, Alexander Mackay. With all the odds against him, he continued, for he knew: "This is where I belong!" I have already mentioned Walter Freytag's visit to a missionary outpost in Upper Egypt where no demonstrable results emerged after 52 years. Yet those missionaries were continuing faithfully, for they knew: "This is where we belong!" So it has always been, and so it will always be.

It was Thursday night, the night before Passover, the night before Calvary. The disciples, wide-eyed and scared, were sitting with Jesus in the upper room, ready to partake of the bread and wine. But the walls of their world were crumbling around them. First Judas left the room, without the others really grasping what was going on. Then Jesus said to Peter, "Before the cock crows twice, you will denounce me three times." To the others he said: "In this night every one of you will take offence at me." In the heart of Thomas, and possibly also others, a thousand questions were raging simultaneously: "Where will this end? Where is this leading to? Who will survive? Who will manage to persevere?" There was so little real understanding in their hearts that the words about His imminent death were an offense. They had visualized it so entirely differently: a king's throne, and places of honor on both sides of the king. Should it surprise us if several had begun to wonder: "Is it possible that we have made a mistake? Suppose He is *not* the Messiah? Suppose we have made the wrong choice?"

In the midst of this electric atmosphere they heard His calm and reassuring voice, "You did not choose me: I chose you. I appointed you to go on and bear fruit, fruit that shall last" (John 15:16). You've got it all wrong; it is not true that you were in a position to choose from a multitude of leaders and a variety of professions and that you then, more or less by accident, chose Me and My ministry. No, it was different. Don't you remember? Peter, you and John and James were busy fishing when I called you. And you, Nathanael, were relaxing in the shade of a fig tree, and Matthew was in his tax-gatherer's office. And there you would still be today had I not chosen and summoned you.

The same applies to us today. We will not survive unless we, too, hear Him saying, "You did not choose me: I
chose you. I appointed you to go on and bear fruit, fruit
that shall last."

Notes

1. Lesslie Newbigin, *The Good Shepherd*. Grand Rapids: Eerdmans, 1977, p. 96.

2. *Ibid.*, p. 98.

3. S. H. Moffet, quoted in *Reformed Ecumenical Synod News Exchange*, Feb. 22, 1972.

4. Quoted in *I A M S News Letter* 11, Nov., 1977, p.13.

5. Cf. the chapter "Towards a Spirituality of the Road" in Adrian Hastings' *Mission and Ministry*. London: Sheed and Ward, 1971, pp. 84-95.

6. Kosuke Koyama, *No Handle on the Cross*. Maryknoll: Orbis Books, 1977, p. 71.

7. *Ibid.*, p. 2.

8. Cf. Horst Baum, *Mut zum Schwachsein-in Christi Kraft*. St. Augustin: Steyler Verlag, 1977, p. 25. I gratefully register my indebtedness to this book for helping to open my eyes to the significance of 2 Corinthians for the understanding of "missionary spirituality."

9. Cf. Baum, *Ibid.*, pp. 160-162, 166, 191.

10. *Confessions* I, 6, quoted by Koyama, *op. cit.*, p. 72.

11. *Ibid.*, p. 75.

12. Cf. J. Comblin, *The Meaning of Mission*. Maryknoll: Orbis Books, 1977, p. 80.

13. Koyama, *op. cit.*, p. 84.

14. *Ibid.*, p. 41.

15. Cf. Baum, *op. cit.*, p. 246.

16. H. Kraemer, *The Christian Message in a Non-Christian World*. London: E H P, 1947, p. 140.

17. Cf. A. J. Dain, *Missionary Candidates*. London: Evangelical Missionary Alliance, 1964, p. 4.

18. Mildred Cable and Francesca French, *Ambassadors for Christ*. Chicago: Moody Press, p. 30.

19. J. A. Loewen, "Self-Exposure: Bridge to Fellowship," *Practical Anthropology* 12:2, March-April 1965, p. 59.

20. Ivan Illich, *Mission and Midwifery*. Gwelo (Rhodesia/Zimbabwe): Mambo Press, 1974, p. 7.

21. Cf. J. Comblin, *op. cit.*, p. 107.

22. "I Am a Stranger in My Father's House," *African Ecclesiastical*

Review 14:3, 1972, pp. 243-253; "I Speak in the House of My Hosts," *Catalyst* 7:2, 1977, pp. 84-105.

23. Cf. Baum, *op. cit.*, p. 234.

24. James Wilkie, "An Essay in Understanding," *International Review of Missions* 219, July 1966, p. 344.

25. Published in Missiology 1:4, Oct. 1973, pp. 405-423.

26. Compare in this connection Horst Baum, *op. cit.*, passim, and J. Comblin, *op. cit.*, especially the chapter "Gospel Mission as Strength in Weakness," pp. 80-87.

27. Comblin, *op. cit.*, p. 81.

28. Cf. Baum, *op. cit.*, p. 168.

29. Cf. L. Newbigin, *op. cit.*, pp. 146, 147.

30. Quoted by Baum, *op. cit.*, p. 210.

31. Koyama, *op. cit.*, p. 37.

32. Cf. Baum, *op. cit.*, p.175.

Missionary Study Series

Published by Herald Press, Scottdale, Pennsylvania, in association with the Institute of Mennonite Studies, Elkhart, Indiana.

1. *The Challenge of Church Growth.* A symposium edited by Wilbert R. Shenk with contributions also from John H. Yoder, Allan H. Howe, Robert L. Ramseyer, and J. Stanley Friesen (1973).

2. *Modern Messianic Movements, as a Theological and Missionary Challenge* by Gottfried Oosterwal (1973).

3. *From Kuku Hill: Among Indigenous Churches in West Africa* by Edwin and Irene Weaver (1975).

4. *Bibliography of Henry Venn's Printed Writings with Index* by Wilbert R. Shenk (1975).

5. *Christian Mission and Social Justice* by Samuel Escobar and John Driver (1978).

6. *A Spirituality of the Road* by David J. Bosch (1979).

7. *Mission and the Peace Witness: The Gospel and Christian Discipleship.* A symposium edited by Robert L. Ramseyer with contributions also from James E. Metzler, Marlin E. Miller, Richard Showalter, Ronald J. Sider, Sjouke Voolstra, and John H. Yoder (1979).

The Missionary Study Series grows out of the Mennonite Missionary Study Fellowship (MMSF) program. The MMSF is an informal fellowship of persons interested in Christian mission, meeting annually for a three-day conference on issues central to their task. It includes missionaries, mission board administrators, theologians, sociologists, and others. It is sponsored by the Institute of Mennonite Studies, 3003 Benham Avenue, Elkhart, Ind. 46514. Books in the series may be ordered from Provident Bookstores, 616 Walnut Avenue, Scottdale, Pa. 15683.

David Jacobus Bosch is a theology professor at the University of South Africa in Pretoria and general secretary of the South African Missiological Society. He brings to mission discussions a wide range of academic and practical missionary experience.

An ordained minister in the Dutch Reformed Church of South Africa, he served as a missionary at Madwaleni, Transkei, from 1957 to 1966. For five years he served as a seminary teacher in Transkei, teaching in church history and missiology.

Bosch has degrees in languages (Dutch, German, Afrikaans) from the University of Pretoria and a doctorate in New Testament from the University of Basel (1956). Since 1972 he has been a member of the faculty of the University of South Africa, serving as dean of the theology faculty from 1974 to 1977. The author of many articles, especially in mission and theology journals, Bosch has also written several books: in German *Die Heidenmission in der Zukunftsschau Jesu* (Zürich, 1959), in Afrikaans *Die lydende Messias en ons sendingmotief* (Pretoria, 1961), and in Dutch *Het evangelie in Afrikaans gewaad* (Kampen, 1975).

Professor Bosch was born in 1929 in Kuruman, Cape Province, South Africa, and is married to Annemarie Roberts. They have six children.